BRITISH NESTING
BIRDS AND
THEIR EGGS

The typography and binding of this book conform to the authorised economy standard.

Printed by Harding & Curtis, Ltd., Bath, and
Published by John Crowther Ltd., Bognor Regis, Sussex.

6/—

Uniform in this Series
by the same Author :-

MAMMALS AND REPTILES OF THE BRITISH ISLES

. . .

TREES AND SHRUBS OF THE BRITISH ISLES

. . .

INSECTS OF THE BRITISH ISLES

. .

FRESH WATER FISH OF THE BRITISH ISLES

BRITISH NESTING BIRDS AND THEIR EGGS

(ILLUSTRATED)

BY

N. BARRIE HODGSON

A GUIDE TO THE
HABITS AND CHARACTERISTICS OF
BRITISH NESTING BIRDS AND THE
IDENTIFICATION OF THEIR EGGS

A
JOHN CROWTHER
PUBLICATION
BOGNOR REGIS
SUSSEX

LIST OF ILLUSTRATIONS.

INTRODUCTION.

THE study of our British nesting birds affords an amount
of interest to those who wish to obtain first hand know-
ledge relating to the habits of the various species by
quietly and patiently watching the birds in their favourite
haunts. It would be difficult to name any part of these
Islands where birds of some description are not found, for
different varieties are adapted to various localities such as
seashore, marshland, downland, wooded districts and around
ponds, lakes and on river banks as well as at great elevations
on mountain sides.

When studying a collection of birds in a museum the beak,
legs, feet, as well as a detailed examination of the colouring
of the plumage is possible, but watching birds in the countryside does not always allow such close inspection. It is
necessary, therefore, to note the general characteristics of
the bird, such as its mode of flight, whether an eater of seeds
or grubs and most important of all, the locality in which the
particular species is seen. Most birds are fond of inhabiting
districts near water but some are essentially water-loving
creatures such as the Reed Warbler, Kingfisher and Coot,
whose nests are always situated among the reeds growing in
a pond or stream or in the herbage at the water's edge;
their food, too, is obtained in, or around ponds which con-
stitutes the reason for their watery haunts. Again, some
birds inhabit the woods and are rarely seen elsewhere while
others prefer the open country, especially downlands which are
well covered with furze and hawthorn bushes in which to
roost and conceal their nests. Notice should be taken of the
surroundings in which each bird is seen as this is helpful to
identification.

Most of the summer migrants arriving on these shores in
the spring are of a shy nature and must be sought in their
wild woodland haunts. Many birds are best observed during
the breeding season, for being much preoccupied in the
construction of the nest and later in feeding their young, they
are less likely to notice that their movements are being

watched. A sharp look out should be kept as soon as the birds are due to arrive as most of them begin nesting very soon after their arrival. In order to make the acquaintance of these numerous summer visitors during the few months they are with us, careful watching will be necessary, for although their song will reveal their presence it is by no means easy to approach near enough to obtain a good view of the bird. Every movement on the part of the observer is watched by these timid creatures and unless one's presence is unknown to them, they will keep at a safe distance. Many of the rarer species may be observed if a favourable site is chosen on the borders of a wood or along a hedgerow where one may have a good view of the neighbouring trees and surrounding bushes. Such a position, if carefully selected, will doubtless bring reward.

The following list is provided to shows at a glance which are the resident birds and which are the summer and winter visitors ; the length, too, of each bird is given to serve as a guide to identification. In the same way a reference to this list will show the average number of eggs laid by each bird, together with the months when nesting is at its height.

LIST OF COMMON BRITISH NESTING BIRDS.

Name of Bird.	Length.	Eggs.	
RAVEN	24 ins.	5-6 March	Resident.
ROOK	19 ins.	3-5 March	Resident.
JACKDAW	14 ins.	3-6 March	Resident.
MAGPIE	18 ins.	6-7 March	Resident
JAY	14 ins.	5-6 April	Resident.
STARLING	8½ ins.	4-6 March— April	Resident and winter visitor.
HAWFINCH ..	7 ins.	3-5 April	Resident.
GREENFINCH ..	6 ins.	4-6 April	Resident.
GOLDFINCH ..	5¼ ins.	4-5 April	Resident.
LINNET	5¾ ins.	4-6 April	Resident.
BULLFINCH ..	6 ins.	4-5 May	Resident.
CHAFFINCH ..	6 ins.	4-5 April— May	Resident.
TREE SPARROW ..	5½ ins.	4-5 April	Resident
HOUSE SPARROW	6 ins.	4-6 April	Resident.
YELLOW BUNTING	6½ ins.	3-5 April	Resident.
SKYLARK	7 ins.	4-5 March	Resident.
TREE PIPIT ..	6 ins.	4-6 May	Summer visitor.
MEADOW PIPIT ..	5¾ ins.	5-6 April	Resident.
PIED WAGTAIL ..	7½ ins.	4-6 April— May	Resident.
REED BUNTING ..	6 ins.	4-5 April— May	Resident.
CHIFF-CHAFF ..	4¾ ins.	6 April— May	Summer visitor.
TREE CREEPER ..	4¾ ins.	6-9 April— May	Resident.
GREAT TIT ..	6 ins.	6-8 May	Resident.
LONG-TAILED TIT	5½ ins.	6-10 May	Resident.
BLUE TIT ..	4½ ins.	7-12 April— May	Resident.
GOLDCREST ..	3½ ins.	6-10 April	Resident.

Name of Bird.	Length.	Eggs.	
BROWN WREN ..	3½ ins.	6-10 March April	Resident.
RED-BACKED SHRIKE	7 ins.	4-7 May	Summer visitor.
WOOD WARBLER	5¼ ins.	5-7 May	Summer visitor.
REED WARBLER	5 ins.	4-5 May	Summer visitor.
SPOTTED FLYCATCHER	5½ ins.	3-5 May	Summer visitor.
BLACKBIRD ..	10 ins.	4-5 March	Resident.
MISSEL THRUSH ..	11 ins.	4-6 February	Resident.
SONG THRUSH ..	9 ins.	4-6 February —March	Resident.
BLACKCAP ..	5½ ins.	5-6 May	Summer visitor.
GREATER WHITE-THROAT	5½ ins.	5-6 May	Summer visitor.
HEDGE SPARROW	5½ ins.	4-6 March	Resident.
ROBIN ,, ..	5¾ ins.	5-6 April	Resident.
NIGHTINGALE ..	6½ ins.	4-6 May	Summer visitor.
STONECHAT ..	5¼ ins.	5-6 April	Resident.
WHINCHAT ..	5¼ ins.	4-6 May	Summer visitor.
WHEATEAR ..	6 ins.	5-7 April— May	Summer visitor.
SWALLOW ..	7½ ins.	4-6 May	Summer visitor.
HOUSE MARTIN ..	5½ ins.	4-5 April— May	Summer visitor.
SAND MARTIN ..	5 ins.	4-6 April— May	Summer visitor.
SWIFT	7 ins.	2 May	Summer visitor.
DIPPER	7 ins.	4-6 April	Resident.
GREEN WOODPECKER	12 ins.	5-7 April	Resident.
LESSER-SPOTTED .. WOODPECKER	6 ins.	6-7 May	Resident.
CUCKOO	13 ins.	May	Summer visitor.
WRYNECK ..	7½ ins.	7-10 May	Summer visitor.
KINGFISHER ..	7½ ins.	6-8 April	Resident.
LONG-EARED OWL	14 ins.	4-6 April	Resident and winter visitor.

Name of Bird.	Length.	Eggs.	
SHORT-EARED OWL	15 ins.	6-8 April	Resident and winter visitor.
TAWNY OWL	15 ins.	3-4 April	Resident.
BARN OWL	14 ins.	2 April	Resident.
SPARROW HAWK	13 ins.	4-6 May	Resident.
HOBBY	12 ins.	3-5 May	Summer visitor.
MERLIN	11 ins.	4-6 April— May	Resident.
KESTREL	14 ins.	4-6 April— May	Resident.
PEREGRIN FALCON	15 ins.	4-6 May	Resident.
POCHARD	19 ins.	7-12 April	Resident and winter visitor.
EIDER DUCK	25 ins.	5-7 April	Resident.
TEAL	15 ins.	8-10 April	Resident and winter visitor.
MALLARD	24 ins.	10-12 April– May	Resident and winter visitor.
SHAG	27 ins.	3-4 May	Resident.
CORMORANT	36 ins.	3-5 May	Resident.
GANNET	33 ins.	1 April— May	Resident.
OYSTER CATCHER	16 ins.	3 April	Resident.
GOLDEN PLOVER	11 ins.	4 April	Resident.
WOOD PIGEON	17 ins.	2 April	Resident.
STOCK DOVE	13 ins.	2 April	Resident.
TURTLE DOVE	11 ins.	2 May	Summer visitor.
LITTLE GREBE	9 ins.	4-6 April— May	Resident.
RED-THROATED DIVER	21 ins.	2 May	Resident and winter visitor.
SANDPIPER	8 ins.	4 April— May	Summer visitor.
REDSHANK	11 ins.	4 April— May	Resident.

Name of Bird.	Length.	Eggs.	
SNIPE	10 ins.	4	April—May	Resident and winter visitor.
LAPWING	12 ins.	4	March—April	Resident.
WOODCOCK	14 ins.	4	March—April	Resident and winter visitor.
COMMON GULL	18 ins.	3	April	Resident.
BLACK-HEADED GULL	16 ins.	3	April	Resident.
COMMON TERN	14½ ins.	3	April	Resident and summer migrant
GUILLEMOT	18 ins.	1	April—May	Resident.
RAZORBILL	17 ins.	1	April	Resident.
PUFFIN	13 ins.	1	April	Summer migrant
MOORHEN	13 ins.	7-9	March—April	Resident.
COOT	15 ins.	7-10	March–April	Resident.
PARTRIDGE	12 ins.	10-15	April	Resident.
GROUSE	16 ins.	8-10	March—April	Resident.
PHEASANT	37 ins.	10-14	April	Resident.

RAVEN (*Corvus corax*).

(Plate 1, fig. 4).

IT is indeed unfortunate that this striking bird has become
so noticeably scarce in recent years, and that many
favourite haunts where once it bred with great regularity,
are now vacated. Only in the wildest, hilly country inland and
along the least inhabited portions of the coast is it still to be
found in England, but in Scotland it is, perhaps, more
commonly observed especially on the islands around the
Scottish coasts. There are still some well-known haunts of
this bird in Ireland and Wales but it is, nevertheless, rare
everywhere.

The Raven, unlike the Rook, is a solitary bird; it may be
seen among the crags and rocks usually in not more than twos
or threes. It is the largest of the Crows being some five inches
longer than the Carrion Crow, Hooded Crow or Rook, and
of a heavy build with a stout bill.

All the Crows possess the same slow, dignified manner and
this characteristic is particularly noticeable in the Raven.
The wing-strokes are slow and when disturbed while feeding
or resting on a ledge of rock it appears to rise with an effort
and soars into the air with a powerful flight. As black is the
predominant colour of this family of birds the various species
are not always distinguishable from one another at a distance,
and unless one is sufficiently experienced at bird watching to
identify these birds by their flight it will be necessary to
observe them at comparatively close quarters in order to
recognize such species by its distinctive colourings or markings.
The Raven may be identified by the entirely black, lustrous
plumage and massive black bill; the feet and legs are also
black and the chief distinguishing feature is the presence of
long, loosely-hanging feathers on the throat. This formation
of feathers is not present in the other Crows. The bill is also
a prominent feature being particularly strong and hooked
which enables the bird to tear to pieces a carcase in a
remarkably short time and, by digging its powerful talons
into the animal, it pulls away the flesh in large pieces swallowing
them in a savage manner.

The cry of the Raven is loud and fearsome and is best described as a deep, hoarse croak uttered frequently, especially during the breeding season when the bird will be observed perched on a prominent piece of rock or cliff swaying as it calls.

The food consists chiefly of fresh killed meat but carrion is the most sought-after meal, and therefore this bird is perhaps most likely to be seen fairly close to when feeding on carrion where several birds will gather together round the carcass of a sheep. The main supply of food is obtained in the form of small animals such as mice, rats, young rabbits as well as small birds. By nature it is shy and will not allow one to approach too near its feeding ground to obtain a close view.

NEST: A massive structure composed of a large amount of sticks sometimes intertwined with tough roots or heather and lined with hair, fur or sheep's wool or similar soft materials. It is usually placed on a ledge of a cliff under the shelter of a piece of over-hanging rock, but the birds which breed inland select a large tree, the nest being placed in the upper branches.

EGGS: Usually 3 to 5 but not uncommonly clutches of 7 are laid; the colouring is greenish-blue, profusely blotched with deep olive green, brown and black. (Plate 1, fig. 4a).

ROOK (*Corvus frugilegus*).

(Plate 1, fig. 2).

This familiar bird is by far the commonest member of the Crow family being found in all parts of the country, for it is equally plentiful on the coast as well as inland.

The general colouring is glossy black with a lustrous purplish sheen; the legs, feet and bill are also black. Unlike the other birds of this order the Rook has a distinguishing feature in the form of a white patch of skin on the face at the base of the bill and although this is not discernible at a distance, it serves as a certain means of identification when the bird is observed close to. This is only present in the adult birds.

The characteristic of these birds is their strong social habits

PLATE I.

1. Jackdaw.
2. Rook.
3. Magpie.
4. Raven.

1a. Egg.
2a. Egg.
3a. Egg.
4a. Egg.

for they roost in companies and move about to fresh feeding grounds in large flocks as well as nesting in a common rookery.

Rooks possess a more vegetarian diet than the other species of Crows and ripe fruit, when in season, has a strong attraction for these birds. During the winter months they may be seen in large flocks on arable land especially when ploughing is in progress, devouring the grubs and various insects in the newly turned soil. On the coast they often appear in numbers on the shore picking up all manner of scraps, for their diet is very varied.

The cry is the familiar harsh " caw " usually repeated three or four times.

Another member of the Crow family closely resembling the Rook is the Carrion Crow which is the same size as the Rook and of similar colouring but without the white patch at the base of the bill and can be distinguished from the latter by its very heavy, slow flight.

NEST: A large structure composed of sticks, coarse grass and roots, and lined with softer materials. Although solitary nests are sometimes observed it is more usual for these birds to breed in companies. The nests are placed in close proximity to each other in the topmost branches of tall trees, particularly elms, the same nests being used year after year, with repairs carried out where necessary.

EGGS: Average number 3 to 4, ground colour greenish blotched with brown, Occasionally laying commences in February, but March is the month when the majority of the birds are sitting. (Plate 1, fig. 2a).

JACKDAW (Corvus mondeula).

(Plate 1, fig. 1).

This bird is the smallest of the Crows and is usually seen in the company of Rooks. From a distance it is not easily distinguishable from the latter birds but may be readily identified when feeding with a flock of Rooks upon the ground by its smaller size and somewhat smarter appearance, as well as by its less dignified movements. The chief colour characteristics consist of the grey neck and nape; the plumage above is black with a purplish-green gloss; the under parts of the body dull black; bill, legs and feet black.

At all times they are social birds living together in communities of varying sizes. The call of the Jackdaw is a shrill, harsh note somewhat resembling the sound "jak" from whence it derives its name.

Although a resident bird, nesting seldom begins before the end of April, that is a month to six weeks later than the Rook.

NEST: Constructed of sticks, dry grass, straw and leaves and lined with fur and wool. Sometimes situated in the branches of a tree but more usually in a hole in a tree or cliff, or crevices in buildings and ruins.

EGGS: 3 to 6 in number, ground colour bluish or greenish white mottled with numerous small brown spots. (Plate 1, fig. 1a).

MAGPIE (*Pica rustica*).

(Plate 1, fig. 3).

Open country and in the vicinity of small copses are the favourite haunts of this bird. It is not often seen near habitations but prefers the wilder regions where it lives usually in small colonies. The Magpie can never be confused with any other British bird for the strongly contrasting black and white plumage, together with the characteristic jaunty movements both in flight and when on the ground, will always supply a means of identification. The long, tapering tail is also a feature of the bird.

The head and back are jet black; the wings black but with numerous streaks and bars of white; under parts of the body white; tail feathers black, marked with blue, green and reddish-brown. The cry is loud and harsh and uttered mostly when the bird is disturbed while feeding or during the breeding season.

Among the great variety of foods relished by the Magpie the chief objects of diet comprise mice, moles, grubs and snails, as well as insects and fruit.

NEST: By no means difficult to detect, being a particularly bulky structure, situated in a small tree or large bush and often very conspicuous owing to the mass of sticks and roots from which it is formed, straggling down from the nest. It is domed with an entrance hole towards the top, and the same nest is often used year after year.

EGGS: 6 to 7 in number, pale greenish-blue, profusely marked with greenish and brownish spots. (Plate 1, fig. 3a).

JAY (*Garrulus glandarius*).
(Plate 2, fig. 1).

The Jay is a common bird but more often heard than seen. Woods are its favourite haunts and when one enters a wood the first crack of a stick underfoot may cause the Jay to utter its warning cry which consists of a particularly harsh screech and on the approach of danger this bird promptly disappears from view into the depths of the wood where only its cry reveals its whereabouts.

It is a brilliantly coloured bird and recognized at once on sight. The plumage of the wings is the most conspicuous part of the Jay, the colours consisting of blue, white and black bars; back reddish; chin white; crest whitish streaked with black; under parts white and the characteristic white breast streaked with black.

NEST: Constructed of twigs and lined with grass and root-fibres; usually placed in the fork of a small tree or at the top of a tall bush.

EGGS: 5 to 6 in number, of a pale bluish-green, profusely, but faintly, speckled with brown. (Plate 2, fig. 1a).

STARLING (*Sturnus vulgaris*).
(Plate 2, fig. 2).

Owing to the habit of these birds of frequenting dwelling houses they are very familiar to town dwellers, in fact they are often observed at closer range in towns and cities than is always possible in the open country. The Starling is a member, or rather, belongs to a sub-family of the Crows and, therefore, from a distance appears a somewhat dull coloured

bird, but on closer examination the plumage is seen to possess the remarkable sheen so characteristic of the Crows. The general colouring is black with distinct reflections of green and purple and a slightly speckled breast. The female has more brownish speckles and is, in appearance, somewhat lighter and more rusty-coloured than the male. The bill in the male is yellow; in the female brownish.

Starlings begin nesting as early as March at which season they indulge in their noisy chatter; they can scarcely be called songsters for they utter a broken, chattering sound which usually betrays their whereabouts.

NEST: Composed of a variety of materials the chief of which consist of hay, straw, moss and small twigs, and lined with wool and feathers. The birds breeding near to habitation build their nests in the eaves of houses and in the rafters of barns and similar well-secluded places, while those inhabiting the open country select a convenient hole in a tree or in a cavity in a bank. The nest is a particularly untidy structure.

EGGS: 4 to 6 in number; pale blue. (Plate 2, fig. 2a).

HAWFINCH (*Coccothraustes vulgaris*).
(Plate 2, fig. 3).

This bird is also known as the Grosbeak and is less likely to be seen than the other members of the Finch family. It is by no means uncommon but its distribution is local, being more plentiful in some districts than in others. It is the largest of the Finches and somewhat resembles the Bullfinch in general build but is one inch longer. When seen for the first time the bull-like neck, large head and massive bill will at once establish its identity, for no other bird possesses a bill as strong and heavily built as this Finch. Such a bill is provided for the purpose of cracking open nuts in order to extract the kernel. Apart from nuts it feeds largely on insects and berries, the latter being sought in gardens during the summer and autumn.

Throat black; neck grey; wings blackish with white markings; back reddish-brown; under parts of the body light reddish-brown.

song is melodious but no great variety of notes is
! and a long drawn-out whistle repeated four or five
ll reveal its whereabouts.

Built of small twigs and lichens, and lined with hair
roots.   The usual site for the nest is in large hawthorn
but any convenient fork in a tree may be chosen
firs and oaks.
3 to 5 in number; pale buff or green, lightly spotted
brown and streaked with grey.   (Plate 2, fig. 3a).

GREENFINCH (*Ligurinus chloris*).
(Plate 2, fig. 4).

Greenfinch is about as common a bird as the Chaffinch
equally well distributed.   The chief means of distinguishing it from the other Finches is by the short, stout bill
and yellowish-green plumage streaked with yellow and grey.
The back, head and neck are olive-green; a yellowish stripe
over the eye; the wings are a darker green as also is the tail,
but the central feathers of the latter are yellow; underparts
of body yellow; bill flesh coloured.   The female is generally
duller, being a more uniform yellowish brown.

During the winter months these birds move about to fresh
feeding-grounds in large flocks and, being seed-eaters, are most
commonly observed on newly-sown fields of corn.   Buds of
various trees also constitute part of their diet as well as many
other kinds of seeds and grain.

NEST: Made from root-fibres, wool and moss, lined with
hair and feathers.   It is compact and beautifully constructed
and usually situated low down in a thick bush or sometimes in
a small tree.

EGGS: 4 to 6 in number; pale bluish-white, blotched with
orange-brown and speckled with dark brown mostly towards
the larger end.   (Plate 2, fig. 4a).

GOLDFINCH (*Fringilla carduelis*).
(Plate 2, fig. 5).

Although not so plentiful as the Chaffinch or Greenfinch

the Goldfinch is, nevertheless, frequently seen in the open country. It is for the most part a seed-eater and has a particular liking for thistle seeds and is, therefore, most likely to be observed in the localities where these plants abound.

At a distance it is easily distinguished by the brilliant patch of gold colour on the wings. The back is dark brown; crown of the head black and a black band from the crown to the shoulders; sides of head white; forehead and throat crimson; wings black with conspicuous yellow or gold and white patches; tail black, tipped with white; under parts of body white; bill dull white with black tip.

The song is sweet if somewhat shrill, consisting of several lively notes.

NEST: Composed of grass, moss and wool, lined with hair and feathers. It is a very compact nest resembling that of the Chaffinch and is often situated in low evergreen bushes but not uncommonly in orchard trees.

EGGS: 4 to 5 in number; bluish-white spotted with reddish-brown, with a few dark brown streaks towards the larger end. (Plate 2, fig. 5a).

LINNET (*Linota cannabina*).
(Plate 3, fig. 1).

The Linnet is a true member of the Finch family and, like the others of its kind, is a well-known songster. The song is not powerful but consists of sweet, flute-like notes, whilst during the breeding season it utters a number of twittering sounds.

The favourite haunt of this bird is on wasteland and commons especially where furze and similar thick, shrub-like bushes are plentiful. During the winter months it is attracted nearer to habitation, but in the summer it is most often seen in wilder localities.

Chestnut-brown is the general colouring of the back; the undersides of the body being dirty white; wings and tail blackish-brown, marked with white; breast red, the forehead and crown have also a reddish tinge; bill short. The bright

PLATE 3.

1. Linnet.
2. Bullfinch.
3. Chaffinch.
4. Tree Sparrow.
5. House Sparrow.

1a. Egg.
2a. Egg.
3a. Egg.
4a. Egg.
5a. Egg.

colouring of the male's plumage is at its best in the breeding season, the colours being duller throughout the remainder of the year.

NEST: Made of fine root-fibres, grass and moss and lined with hair and feathers; usually situated in a furze bush but not uncommonly found low-down in a thorn-bush.

EGGS: 4 to 6 in number; pale bluish-white spotted with light reddish-brown.   (Plate 3, fig. 1a).

BULLFINCH (*Pyrrhula vulgaris*).
(Plate 3, fig. 2.).

The Bullfinch is fairly well distributed throughout the country and is most commonly found in well-wooded districts. It is rarely observed singly but usually in pairs, or small flocks, and during the winter months is often seen near habitation but in the summer it keeps more to the woods.

The song takes the form of a simple whistle, very rich and clear in tone.

The diet is largely vegetarian consisting of seeds, young immature buds and fruit, the latter often being sought in gardens and orchards.   Insects also comprise no small part of the food of this bird.

The plumage on the upper parts is smoky-grey ; head, including chin, black; wings black with bold white cross-bar; tail black; bill short and thick and blackish; under parts of body, including breast, red.   The female possesses a dark capped head but this is dark brown instead of black; breast pale brown; remainder of plumage generally brownish.

NEST: Constructed on a platform of twigs and composed of finely interwoven root-fibres, lined with hair.   Situated either in a thick whitethorn bush or in a tree well hidden among the foliage.

EGGS: 4 to 5 in number; pale blue well speckled with reddish-brown and streaked with purplish-brown.   (Plate 3, fig. 2a).

CHAFFINCH (*Fringilla coelebs*).
(Pate 3, fig. 3).

This bird may well be described as the commonest of the smaller British song birds and when endeavouring to identify it, care must be taken not to confuse it with the Bullfinch. It is a trifle smaller than the latter and the markings on the plumage differ considerably in detail except for the reddish breast.

Back chestnut-brown; crown and nape slate-grey; forehead black; wings black with two conspicuous white cross-bars; tail black, with the two centre feathers grey and bold white edging to the outer feathers; breast red; under parts of body whitish. In the female the crown and back are olive-brown; under parts olive-grey.

The song is very sweet if a trifle monotonous, a constantly repeated " tweet—tweet—tweet." When alarmed it utters a loud " pick-pick." The song is usually uttered from a prominent branch. During the winter months Chaffinches are often observed in small flocks usually consisting of one sex only.

NEST: Composed of moss, covered with lichens and lined with hair and feathers. The nest is very compact and placed in the fork of a tree or in a large bush.

EGGS: 4 to 5 in number; pale greyish-blue with large blotches of purplish-brown and clouded with pale reddish-brown. (Plate 3, fig. 3a).

TREE SPARROW (*Passer montanus*).
(Plate 3, fig. 4).

This bird, unlike the Hedge Sparrow, is a true member of the well-known Sparrow family and, apart from being a trifle smaller, closely resembles in appearance the House Sparrow. It is similar, too, in general colouring but may be distinguished by the chestnut-brown head and the white patches on the neck and breast. Two white bars are conspicuous on the wings. The female differs in appearance little from the male. This species of Sparrow is less abundant than its cosmopolitan cousin; it is somewhat local in distribution.

The note is like that of the House Sparrow but louder and more shrill.

NEST: Built of hay and well lined with feathers. The nesting site is usually selected in a hole in a decaying tree but various situations such as under the thatch of an old barn or crevices in rocks may be utilized.

EGGS: 4 to 5 in number; greyish-white and very profusely mottled with various shades of brown. (Plate 3, fig. 4a).

HOUSE SPARROW (*Passer domesticus*).
(Plate 3, fig. 5).

Perhaps the most familiar bird in the country and well distributed throughout the British Isles living mostly in close proximity to dwelling houses both in towns as well as in country districts though not so frequently seen in the open country. Its food is very varied, consisting of seeds, insects, corn and any scraps it can find. In cities it frequents dwellings—which afford suitable nesting sites—and where there exists a plentiful supply of scraps of various kinds, while in country districts the chief haunts of the House Sparrow are around farm buildings.

In the male the back is chestnut-brown, inclined to grey towards the tail; the throat and breast black; under parts of body light ash-grey. The head is ash-grey mottled with brown with a whitish patch on the cheeks and sides of the neck. In the female the breast and throat are grey in place of the black.

NEST: Composed of dry grass and straw and well lined with feathers. The favourite nesting sites for these birds which inhabit towns are under the eaves of houses. The nests are very untidy structures,the entrances of which may often be detected by pieces of straw and hay hanging down from the nest. In country districts the nest is most often built in the rafters of a barn or under the eaves of farm buildings, but where no such sites are available a hole in a tree is used.

EGGS: 5 to 6 in number; dirty white, blotched and spotted with varying shades of brown. (Plate 3, fig. 5a).

YELLOW BUNTING (*Emberiza citrinella*).
(Plate 4, fig. 1).

The Yellow Bunting or Yellowhammer is much the commonest of the Buntings, inhabiting hedgerows and therefore being most often seen in lanes, perched on a prominent branch on a hedge. As few British birds possess such a large amount of yellow in their plumage it is easily recognised.

The under parts are yellow, slightly spotted with red and the upper parts yellowish-brown; the head and neck orange. The female is less brightly coloured, being a reddish-brown and the spots on the breast and under parts less distinct.

The song is distinctive and is likened to the familiar " Little bit of bread and no cheese," the last word being drawn out.

The food consists largely of seeds, most of which are obtained on the ground.

NEST: Made of dry grass, lined with hair sometimes situated in low bushes but more usually placed in ditch-sides or on a bank beneath clumps of grass.

EGGS: 3 to 5 in number; purplish-white, streaked and spotted with purplish-brown. (Plate 4, fig. 1a).

SKYLARK (*Alauda arvensis*).
(Plate 4, fig. 2).

The song alone of this bird is sufficient to identify the species but a description may be given for the purpose of recognizing the Skylark when not in song but observed on the ground.

The head and neck are reddish-brown well streaked and mottled with light and dark brown, while the under parts of the body are lighter, being yellowish with fewer and paler brownish streaks; throat and breast whitish with dark streaks; chief wing-feathers edged with white, this latter being very conspicuous when the bird is in flight; central tail feathers dark, outer ones white.

During the winter Larks may often be observed in flocks moving from field to field in search of food which consists largely of seeds and insects. They are never known to roost in trees but when not in the air live entirely on the ground and, therefore, possess feet which are particularly well adapted for the purpose.

Nest: Made of dry grass, lined with finer grass, and always situated on the ground in a meadow or on wasteland, beneath a tuft of grass.

Eggs: 4 to 5 in number; greyish-brown speckled thickly with dark brown. (Plate 4, fig. 2a).

TREE PIPIT (*Anthus trivialis*).
(Plate 4, fig. 3).

The name of this bird aptly describes its habits for it is a bird of the woodlands most usually seen perched on the branches of a tree on the edge of a wood, this characteristic distinguishing it from the Meadow Pipit which resorts chiefly to the open country and lives for the most part upon the ground. Unlike the latter bird the Tree Pipit is commonest in the southern half of the country as it is a summer migrant only and is comparatively scarce in the north. Apart from its habit of living in trees it is not easily distinguished from the Meadow Pipit, being only a quarter of an inch longer with the general colouring and markings very similar; the main differences are, however, a somewhat brighter colouring of the plumage and a flatter crown to the head.

The upper parts are pale brown, the wings having a double whitish wing-bar and the main feathers of the wings, as well as the tail, are dark brown, with the outer tail-feathers white; the under parts are very pale buff spotted with deep brown.

Like the Meadow Pipit the song is often uttered when the bird is in flight and consists of a series of sounds resembling " tee-u tee-u " repeated many times, the song concluding with a long drawn-out " r-ee."

Nest: Constructed of dry grass, fine root-fibres and moss, and lined with very fine grass and hair; situated on the ground beneath a tuft of grass.

Eggs: 4 to 6 in number; ground colour pale buffish-white, finely mottled all over with reddish-brown. (Plate 4, fig. 3a).

MEADOW PIPIT (*Anthus pratensis*).

(Plate 4, fig. 4).

This bird is most commonly found in the north of England and in Scotland and is, as a rule, generally more scarce in the south, where it is often a winter visitor, returning to its northern haunts during the breeding season. It is closely related to the Tree Pipit but this latter bird is a summer visitor only. Ploughed fields are a likely spot to observe the Meadow Pipit, and heaths, downs and commons are also favoured localities. The song is not loud but very attractive.

The plumage is sombre coloured being dull greenish-grey above, mottled with brown and whitish under parts, also spotted with brown. Wing feathers have pale edgings; central tail feathers dark, outer ones white.

NEST: Built of dry grass, lined with finer grass and hair, and always situated on the ground under the shelter of a large tuft of grass.

EGGS: 5 to 6 in number; greyish-white or greenish-white and mottled all over with dark brown. (Plate 4, fig. 4a).

PIED WAGTAIL (*Motacilla alba*).

(Plate 4, fig. 5).

This Wagtail is the commonest and, therefore, more often observed than the Grey and Yellow Wagtails; the last-named being a summer visitor only, usually arriving on these shores in late March. The characteristic contrasting black and white markings of this bird render identification comparatively simple during the summer months but the winter plumage differs in respect to the black markings, these being of an ash-grey. The unusually long tail which constantly " wags " up and down as the bird moves about the ground will also assist in its recognition.

Back, crown of head and collar black; tail black but outside feathers edged with white; sides of face and forehead white, underparts of body white.

PLATE 4.

1.	Yellow Bunting.	1a.	Egg.
2.	Skylark.	2a.	Egg.
3.	Tree Pipet.	3a.	Egg.
4.	Meadow Pipet.	4a.	Egg.
5.	Pied Wagtail.	5a.	Egg.
6.	Reed Bunting.	6a.	Egg.

When on the ground it walks or runs very rapidly and stopping abruptly only pausing a short while, it continues to run hither and thither. Its favourite haunt is by the water's edge where flies and other winged insects are plentiful.

NEST: Constructed of dry grass, moss and fine root-fibres and lined with hair and feathers, placed in a hole in a wall or bank, or other well secluded retreat.

EGGS: 4 to 6 in number; greyish-white, spotted all over with brown and dark grey. (Plate 4, fig. 5a).

REED BUNTING (*Emberiza schoeniclus*).
(Plate 4, fig. 6).

Although, as the name suggests, this bird is found among the reeds, it is also seen on almost any water courses and marsh-land, and may be at once distinguished by its bright coloured plumage, for the other small birds dwelling in these surround-ings, such as the Sedge Warbler and Reed Warbler, are entirely different in markings and have a much more sombre plumage.

The head and throat of the Reed Bunting are black and round the neck is a conspicuous white collar and a pure white streak running from the base of the bill to the white collar; the back is reddish-brown, heavily mottled with black streaks; wing and tail feathers dark brown, the outer feathers of the latter edged with white; under parts of body white, streaked with black. The female differs quite a lot from the male, being generally more brownish and without the black head and white collar.

It seldom resorts to trees but flits about among the reeds and low herbage around a pond, stream and on marshland, uttering a clear song the notes of which are simply a series of " trit-trit-trit,"

NEST: Made mostly of dry grass and small aquatic plants, and lined with very fine root-fibres and grass. Usually situated in a tuft of rushes just above the surface of the water, but not uncommonly placed in low herbage at the water's edge.

EGGS: 4 to 6 in number, of a purplish-grey, streaked and spotted with dark purplish brown. (Plate 4, fig. 6a).

CHIFF-CHAFF (*Phylloscopus rufus*).
(Plate 5, fig. 1).

The Chiff-Chaff is very similar both in size and colouring to the Willow Wren and Wood Wren, and is not easily distinguished except at fairly close quarters, the best means of establishing its identity is by its song. This consists of shrill notes uttered very persistently and resembling the bird's name—" Chiff-chaff." Being one of the first arrivals in the spring the Chiff-Chaff may be heard as early as March, uttering its song in oak woods which appear to be its favourite haunts. It sings full-throatedly on its arrival and again during the weeks preceeding its departure in late September or during October.

The colouring is dull olive-green, tinged with yellow and an indistinct yellowish stripe above the eye; the under parts of the body are dull yellowish white; feet and legs blackish.

NEST: Composed of dry grass, leaves and moss, and lined with feathers. It is a domed structure with an entrance hole at the side and usually situated on, or near the ground, or in a bank bordering a wood. Occasionally in a low bush.

EGGS: 4 to 6 in number; white, spotted with purplish-brown at the larger end. (Plate 5, fig. 1a).

TREE CREEPER (*Certhia familiaris*).
(Plate 5, fig. 2).

From the length of this bird, 5 inches, it will be realized that it is a small creature, its haunts being the woods. Its name suggests the method it employs when hunting for food by creeping round the trunk and branches of trees in search of insects, and it is while so engaged that this bird is most likely to be seen. From a distance it has the appearance of a mouse from its quick movements; the claws are specially adapted for clinging to the bark and its tail is used as a means of support when spread out and pressed against the tree.

Its diet consists almost entirely of insects and their larvae which live on, or under, the bark, and in order to assist in procuring these it is possessed of a very sharp and slightly hooked bill.

The general colour of the plumage is dark brown above, slightly mottled with lighter brown and brownish-white beneath. A pure white streak appears above the eye.

The song is not loud and consists of only a few notes, but the high-pitched, loud call-note is much more likely to attract attention.

NEST: Composed of small twigs, grass and often fragments of decayed wood, with a substantial lining of moss and feathers. A hole in a tree is nearly always the site selected for the nest and it is by no means easily detected.

EGGS: 6 to 9 in number; roundish in shape; pure white, spotted with reddish-brown at the larger end. (Plate 5, fig. 2a).

GREAT TIT (*Parus major*).
(Plate 5, fig. 3).

The Great Tit is the largest of the British Titmice and is not often seen near habitation, as is the case with the Blue and Long-tailed Tits, its favourite haunts being well-wooded districts. In common with the other members of this family it feeds on insects which it hunts on the branches of bushes and trees. It has a particularly cheerful song but no great variety of notes is produced and the result is, therefore, somewhat monotonous.

It is arrayed in very bright plumage which enables it to be recognized easily. Olive-green is the predominent colouring on the upper parts, while the undersides of the body are yellowish; the throat and head are black with a distinct white patch on the cheeks; the wings and tail bluish with several white bars on each; bill unusually short.

NEST: Very similar to that of the Blue Tit and is constructed of fine grass and moss, and lined with hair and feathers. The Great Tit builds its nest in any convenient well-concealed situation such as a hole in a tree or a crevice in a wall; sometimes it uses the old nest of some other bird as a foundation.

PLATE 5.

1. Chiff-Chaff.	1a. Egg.
2. Tree Creeper.	2a. Egg.
3. Great Tit.	3a. Egg.
4. Long-tailed Tit.	4a. Egg.
5. Blue Tit.	5a. Egg.

EGGS: 6 to 8 in number; white, faintly spotted with reddish-brown. (Plate 5, fig. 3a).

LONG-TAILED TIT (*Parus caudatus*).
(Plate 5, fig. 4).

Less common than the familiar Blue Tit but, like the latter bird, is often seen near habitation. In the countryside it is often observed while feeding, for, although it is partial to various scraps, its food consists chiefly of insects which are sought on the twigs and branches as well as on the trunks of trees. The manner in which this bird clings upside down on the tips of the branches hunting for its food, together with its unusually long tail it will be recognized quite easily. It is always more in evidence during the winter months when the branches are bare of foliage and when it is also attracted nearer to habitation in search of food.

The plumage is gery distinctly marked, in contrasting colours; the back and wings are black as also are the head, neck and breast; the tail black, edged with white and the under parts of the body reddish-white.

NEST: Composed of moss, small leaves and lichen, profusely lined with feathers. The nest of the Long-tailed Tit is a particularly beautiful structure, long and domed, with a small entrance hole towards the top; usually situated in a furze bush or thick hedge, but always well concealed.

EGGS: 6 to 10 in number; white, speckled with reddish-brown towards the larger end. (Plate 5, fig. 4a).

BLUE TIT (*Parus cacruleus*).
(Plate 5, fig. 5).

Known also as the Tomtit, this lively little bird is the most familiar of the Titmouse family. It is fond of coming near dwelling houses and, therefore, most frequently observed near habitation during the winter months.

It is impossible to confuse the bird with the others of its kind owing to the predominance of blue colouring in its plumage. The back and wings are bluish inclined to olive-and the tail is also blue. The head is very distinctly marked; a blue crown almost entirely encircled with white and a patch of white on the cheeks.

The food is largely composed of insects and the means by which the bird clings to the tips of the branches, usually upside down, is very characteristic of its species.

The song is not loud but consists of an often repeated trill.

NEST: Very small and exquisitely constructed of moss and hair. The nest sites vary considerably; a hole in a tree is a favourite choice but holes and crevices in walls are, perhaps, the most often selected situations.

EGGS: 7 to 12 in number, sometimes more; white, speckled at the larger end with brown. (Plate 5, fig. 5a).

GOLDCREST (*Regulus christatus*).
(Plate 6, fig. 1).

This is the smallest British bird and not often seen away from its favourite haunts in the pine woods and fir copses. Being of a timid nature it finds in such environment ample security and shelter among the evergreen branches and in thickets surrounding the wood.

The surest means of distinguishing this species from the Common or Brown Wren is by the characteristic crest on the head which is of a bright orange colour. The upper parts of the bird are olive-brown and yellow and pale brownish-grey on the under parts.

The Goldcrest is always much more in evidence during the winter months for it is then that its numbers are greatly increased by a large migration from the Continent.

Insects comprise the chief food of the Goldcrest and these it obtains on the fir trees.

NEST: Composed of moss and lichens and lined with very fine hairs and feathers. It is deep and very compact and usually suspended beneath a branch of fir or against a tree well covered with ivy.

EGGS: 6 to 10 in number; very pale buff, minutely spotted with reddish-brown at the larger end. (Plate 6, fig. 1a).

BROWN WREN (*Troglodytes parvulus*).
(Plate 6, fig. 2).

This familiar little bird is found everywhere throughout the British Isles. It is quick of movement and more often observed during the winter when the trees and bushes are bare of foliage. The Brown or Common Wren, is a familiar creature near habitation yet equally numerous in thickets and woodlands.

The characteristic short, plump body and upturned tail make it easily recognized; the coluring above is reddish-brown with numerous darker brown markings; breast, throat and face whitish, also whitish stripe over the eye; sides of body reddish-brown, barred with dark brown; legs lighter brown and under parts pale brown with dark markings; bill brown, sharply pointed.

The song of the Wren is wonderfully loud for so small a bird, the notes being very clear and rich in tone and consisting of a rapid warble concluding with a series of rattling, mechanical notes.

NEST: Made of grass, leaves and moss, the interior lined with feathers. The nest is domed with a hole in one side towards the top just large enough to allow the bird to enter. It is usually well concealed in a hole in a tree or hidden in the ivy on a tree trunk or against a wall.

EGGS: 6 to 10 in number; white, sometimes plentifully spotted with brown and sometimes with practically no markings at all. (Plate 6, fig. 2a).

RED-BACKED SHRIKE (*Lanius colluris*).
(Plate 6, fig. 3).

This bird is generally seen in hedgerows and in localities where bramble bushes are plentiful and it is much less common in the open country. A summer migrant it arrives early in May; it is fairly common in the southern half of England, becoming scarcer in Yorkshire and rare in Scotland; fairly well distributed in Wales but absent in Ireland.

Its food consists largely of insects which it " spears " on the thorns of a bush, and for this reason has been termed the

PLATE 6.

1.	Goldcrest.	1a. Egg.
2.	Brown Wren.	2a. Egg.
3.	Red-backed Shrike.	3a. Egg.
4.	Wood Warbler.	4a. Egg.
5.	Reed Warbler.	5a. Egg.
6.	Spotted Flycatcher.	6a. Egg.

Butcher Bird. As well as insects, small birds, rodents and frogs are often found on thorns in the proximity of the nest.

The back is red or chestnut-brown; the under parts buff. The head and nape bluish-grey; a broad, conspicuous black band on the side of the face; wings dark brown; tail black but base of feathers white. In the female the upper parts are brown; under parts light brown, barred with darker brown. Apart from the red back in the male, the distinguishing feature of this bird is the hawk-like bill, the tip of the upper mandible being hooked well over the lower.

NEST: Composed of grass, root-fibres and moss, and lined with hair and wool and usually well concealed in a bush but on occasions is situated in a small tree.

EGGS: 4 to 7 in number; bluish-white with brownish spots at the larger end. (Plate 6, fig. 3a).

WOOD WARBLER (*Phylloscopus sibilatrix*).
(Plate 6, fig. 4).

The Wood Warbler or Wood Wren is a typical woodland bird having a particular preference for beech and oak woods. In size and general appearance it resembles the Chiff-Chaff and Willow Wren but is a trifle longer than these last-named birds and possesses a more brightly coloured plumage. Its arrival in the spring is later than that of the Chiff-Chaff for it seldom makes an appearance before the end of April. Although well distributed, the Wood Wren is not so often seen owing to its shy disposition and love of concealed places among the upper brances of a tree, but it can best be observed while hunting for insects on the leaves at the end of a branch.

The song is very sweet but composed of no great variety of notes, the chief call being a clear " Ting."

The plumage is yellowish-green on the upper parts and a bold yellow eye-streak; the throat is bright yellow and the under parts of the body white; feet and legs pale brown.

NEST: Composed of dry grass and lined with hair; domed with an entrance hole at the side and placed on the ground either among tufts of grass or dead leaves.

EGGS: 5 to 7 in number; white, thickly spotted with reddish-brown and grey. (Plate 6, fig. 4a).

REED WARBLER (*Sylvia arundinacea*).
(Plate 6, fig. 5).

This particularly interesting member of the Warbler family is not an early arrival to these shores. It comes from Africa and in some seasons it is well into May before its presence is observed.

A small clump of rushes situated in a large pond or stream is the favourite haunt of this Warbler which may be seen darting around the reeds in search of insects. Although an alternative diet is berries this bird is seldom met with far from its waterside haunts.

The song is particularly sweet but not strong.

Much the most interesting point about this nest is its peculiar construction, it is composed of grasses and suspended among the reeds; long pieces of grass being wound round the latter and interwoven with the nest. In windy weather the reeds are often bent right over, but the nest is unusually deep in construction which saves the eggs from rolling out. When the bird is sitting she is completely concealed within the nest.

Head, nape and back ruddy-brown; wings and tail dark brown, with the edgings to the feathers lighter; under parts of body buffish-white.

NEST: Composed of grass and reeds.

EGGS: 4 to 5 in number; pale greenish-white, finely mottled with olive-brown. (Plate 6, fig. 5a).

SPOTTED FLYCATCHER (*Muscicapa grisola*).
(Plate 6, fig. 6).

One of the later summer arrivals and well distributed throughout the southern half of the country. Owing to the fact that it possesses no song it does not, therefore, attract attention to itself in any way; only very occasionally it utters a curious, rather hoarse cry. From a distance it appears an insignificant little bird but when seen closer to, the spotted breast will serve as a means of identification.

The back, head, wings and tail are greyish-brown, and the breast and underparts greyish-white; the spots on the breast are dark brown.

As its name suggests it feeds on insects which it catches on the wing.

NEST: Made of fine grasses, moss and lichens and lined with feathers, hair and wool. Flycatchers are particularly fond of building their nests in a garden, selecting a site in a creeper or vine against a wall, or in an outbuilding; when away from habitation the favourite situation is usually in the ivy on a tree trunk or sometimes in the fork of a tree.

EGGS: 3 to 5 in number; bluish or greyish-white, spotted and blotched with violet-grey and light brown. (Plate 6, fig. 6a).

BLACKBIRD (*Turdus merula*).
(Plate 7, fig. 1).

The Blackbird is a member of the Thrush family and, apart from its colouring, resembles the Song Thrush in size and appearance to a remarkable degree for it is exceedingly smart, and tidy in its habits. The song is truly as melodious as that of the Thrush but can only be described as possessing a somewhat more cheerful tone and having a lesser variety of notes.

The most favoured haunt of the Blackbird is in the vicinity of shrubs and thick edges; on the approach of danger it utters its well-known warning cry, and flying just over the tops of the bushes, seeks refuge in a dense hedgerow. For this reason these birds are less likely to be seen in the open country where little shelter is available.

The dark plumage of the male and bright orange bill enables immediate identification of this species, but the female does not possess such dark colouring and must not, therefore be confused with the Thrush when seen at a distance.

NEST: Constructed of dry grass lined with finer grass. Unlike the nests of the Missel and Song Thrushes that of the

41

PLATE 7.

1.	Blackbird.	1a.	Egg.
2.	Missel Thrush.	2a.	Egg.
3.	Song Thrush.	3a.	Egg.
4.	Blackcap.	4a.	Egg.
5.	Greater Whitethroat.	5a.	Egg.

Blackbird is not lined with mud. It is usually situated in low bushes and fairly well concealed.

EGGS: 4 to 5 in number; bluish-green, extensively mottled with darker green and blotched with greenish-brown. (Plate 7, fig. 1a).

MISSEL THRUSH (*Tardus viscivorus*).
(Plate 7, fig. 2).

This bird so closely resembles the familiar Song Thrush in general appearance that a fairly close inspection is necessary to identify it when it is perched on the bough of some wayside tree. When in flight, however, it is easily recognised by the distinctive white marking on the under wing-coverts and white streaks on the tail.

The upper parts of the body, including the head, are brown; under parts buffish; breast whitish, heavily marked with dark brown spots.

The song of the Missel Thrush is the surest means of distinguishing it from the Song Thrush, for it utters brief passages with considerable intervals between each; the notes are less sustained and the rich, liquid quality of the latter species is lacking. It is our largest British song bird and one of the earliest to be heard in the spring.

NEST: Made of dry grass, moss and wool and lined with finer grass; like the Song Thrush the nest has a mud lining but this is usually covered with fine grass. The nest is seldom concealed in thickets but more often placed in a fork of a tree and is a bulky structure. Nesting commences as early as February, and two broods are reared in the season.

EGGS: 4 to 5 in number; dirty greenish-white, streaked and blotched with brown, reddish and purplish markings. (Plate 7, fig. 2).

SONG THRUSH (*Turdus musicus*).
(Plate 7, fig. 3).

This is the commonest member of the Thrush family and found in all parts of the British Isles. The song of this bird is, perhaps, the most familiar of any songster and the rich, melodious notes contrast well with the more melancholy song of the Missel Thrush. Being much more common than the last-named bird, it is, therefore, more often seen in almost every locality.

The colouring above is dark brown and lighter on the under parts of the body, but with the absence of the white markings characteristic to the Missel Thrush, except for a lightish patch in the middle of the throat; the speckled breast has a large number of small markings somewhat less clearly defined than the other Thrush.

NEST: Made of dry grass with a substantial mud lining. It is usually situated in a fairly concealed site and often near the ground in a thick bush or less seldom in a small tree. The nesting season begins as early as late February in favourable seasons and continues until quite late in the spring for it is not uncommon for these birds to produce three broods in one season and a separate nest is usually built for rearing each brood.

EGGS: 4 to 6 in number; clear blue, sparsely spotted with dark brown towards the larger end and a trifle smaller in size than those of the Missel Thrush. (Plate 7, fig. 3a).

BLACKCAP (*Sylvia atricapilla*).
(Plate 7, fig. 4).

A small bird, much more often heard than seen for, owing to its shy nature, it resorts to thick bramble bushes and there, well concealed, pours forth its particularly beautiful and melodious song; it is seldom heard in woods but haunts chiefly hedgerows and commons. Although a summer visitor to these shores it is reported sometimes to remain with us during the winter in the south of England.

It is easily recognised by its jet black head, resembling a cap. The rest of the body is ashy-grey except for a whitish tinge on the belly. The female has a more brownish head and the body more generally brown than the male.

NEST: Composed of fine grasses and root-fibres and lined with similar materials. The nest is built in early May and

44

situated low down in a thick bush, the most favourite being bramble or wild rose. It is a particularly frail structure.

Eggs: 5 to 6 in number; pale grey with numerous dark brown markings. (Plate 7, fig. 4).

GREATER WHITETHROAT (*Sylvia cinerea*).
(Plate 7, fig. 5).

This is the larger of the two Whitethroats, the other species being the Lesser Whitethroat. The Greater Whitethroat or Common Whitethroat as it is also called is much commoner than its near relative and certainly more often seen; both species possess very similar habits and there is no marked distinction in the colouring of the plumage.

The song is too harsh to be called sweet but, on occasions, it utters a short strain of not at all an unpleasant character. A distinctive feature of this bird is its unusual mode of flight which is made up of a series of jerky movements in an up and down direction as though the bird were flying against a very strong wind. Common-land well covered with thick bushes, as well as hedgerows, are the most favourite haunts of the Greater Whitethroat.

The back and wings are reddish-brown; the under parts whitish; throat pure white and the head grey. The female is very similar to the male, the white being slightly more greyish.

Nest: Composed of fine grasses and root-fibres, lined with fine grass. It is a loosely-built, frail structure often situated near the ground in a clump of nettles or sometimes in a bramble bush.

Eggs: 5 to 6 in number; greenish, spotted with brown and grey. (Plate 7, fig. 5a).

HEDGE SPARROW (*Accentor modularis*).
(Plate 8, fig. 1).

This bird is no relation whatever to the very familiar House Sparrow but is a member of the Thrush family and, unlike the House Sparrow, has a delightful song and is a

PLATE 8.

1.	Hedge Sparrow.	1a.	Egg.
2.	Robin.	2a.	Egg.
3.	Nightingale.	3a.	Egg.
4.	Stonechat.	4a.	Egg.
5.	Whinchat.	5a.	Egg.
6.	Wheatear.	6a.	Egg.

very active creature of neat appearance. Apart from the difference in colouring of plumage, the Hedge Sparrow may be distinguished from the House Sparrow by its slender beak. It feeds chiefly on seeds and insects.

The back and wings are brown with reddish-brown markings, while the head and neck have well-defined dark brown streaks; under parts of body dull white; legs flesh coloured.

Nesting begins in March and there are at least two and often three broods in the season.

NEST: Made of fine grasses and moss, lined with hair and placed in hedgerows and bramble bushes.

EGGS: 4 to 6 in number; light blue. (Plate 8, fig. 1a).

ROBIN (*Sylvia rubecula*).
(Plate 8, fig. 2).

The Robin or Redbreast is so well known that a description is scarcely necessary, but the young of this species differ so considerably from the adult birds that it is not an uncommon thing to mistake them for other varieties of birds. The familiar red breast of the adult bird is not present in the young one, for their breasts are spotted like the Thrush, for which they might easily be mistaken.

The adult female is similar to the male with the exception of the breast which is of a slightly paler red.

Often on a winter's day, when all other song birds are silent, the Robin is uttering his very sweet but somewhat plaintive song.

NEST: Composed of dry grass, moss and leaves, lined with hair and sometimes a few feathers. No particular nesting site can be named but well-concealed spots such as in haystacks or outbuildings, or even in an old can, a nest may be found, as well as among ivy on a tree trunk or wall, or in a bank.

EGGS: 5 to 6 in number; white, delicately speckled with light reddish-brown. (Plate 8, fig. 2a).

NIGHTINGALE (*Sylvia luscinia*).
(Plate 8, fig. 3).

Of all the British song-birds the Nightingale is, perhaps, the best known because of its nocturnal song. It sings by day as well as at night but the song is not so easily distinguished when other songsters are pouring forth their individual strains.

The Nightingale belongs to the Thrush family and is not unlike a small Song Thrush in appearance and general habits. The head, back and wings are chestnut-brown and the breast and under parts of the body a dull whitish colour; the tail dark reddish-brown and slightly forked. The plumage of the female bird is similar to that of the male.

It is very local in distribution, being quite common in some parts while in other districts it is never heard. Year after year it returns to its favourite haunts in some quiet wood or small copse or well sheltered garden. It is much more plentiful in the southern counties of England although it is by no means absent as far north as Scotland.

NEST: Composed chiefly of dead leaves, lined with fine grass; nearly always situated in a thick bush close to the ground. It is skilfully built and exceedingly difficult to detect for if not made entirely of leaves, the outside of the nest is always covered with a quantity of dead leaves.

EGGS: 4 to 6 in number; plain olive-brown. (Plate 8, fig. 3a).

STONECHAT (*Saxicola rubicola*).
(Plate 8, fig. 4).

This bird is not uncommon around the coast, but inland seems to be confined mostly to commons and wasteland where furze bushes abound. It is of a timid nature and most often seen perched on the topmost branch of a bush in full view and darting into the thickest part of the foliage when danger is suspected.

The song is monotonous and somewhat plaintive in character. The food consists entirely of insects.

The head is black with a patch of black on the throat; back, wings and tail black; breast reddish-brown; under parts whitish. The female is not nearly so handsomely clad as the male.

Although a resident bird it seldom begins nesting before early May.

NEST: Made of dry grass and moss, lined with hair and feathers; it is a beautiful little nest very delicately constructed and situated on the ground at the roots of a furze or other thick bush.

EGGS: 5 to 6 in number; pale blue, delicately spotted with reddish-brown at the larger end. (Plate 8, fig. 4a).

WHINCHAT (*Saxicola rubetra*).
(Plate 8, fig. 5).

This small summer visitor is not an early arrival often appearing as late as the beginning of May. Seldom is it seen near habitation, for it frequents furze commons and wild stretches of heath where it may be seen flitting from bush to bush with an undulating flight, and usually remaining well concealed except when singing. Perched on the topmost branch of a bush it utters its persistent and melodious song. Its diet is composed entirely of insects.

The upper parts of the body are yellowish-brown, somewhat darker on the crown of the head, with a very distinct patch of white over the eye; a whitish patch also occurs on the sides of the neck and in the middle of the wings; breast reddish and the under parts yellow-white. The female is without the white on the wings, and the white streak over the eye is far less prominent.

NEST: Composed of dry grass and fine root-fibres, lined with hair and wool; the most favourite nesting-site is in a furze bush, close to the ground.

EGGS: 4 to 6 in number; usually plain greenish-blue but sometimes with small purplish speckles at the larger end. (Plate 8, fig. 5a).

WHEATEAR (*Saxicola aenanthe*).

(Plate 8, fig. 6).

The favourite haunts of the Wheatear are in wild situations such as downs, mountain sides and heaths; it will be observed most commonly sitting on a stone or similar prominent object from which it can obtain a good view of the insects in the air. At intervals it will dart upwards seizing its prey and returning to the stone where it awaits another tempting morsel to come its way.

The song is soft and therefore not easily distinguished in the open country in which the bird is usually observed.

The colouring of the back, crown and hind-neck is bluish-grey; a streak of white over the eye; very conspicuous black stripe through the eye; wings black; tail black but with white tips to outer feathers; throat and breast buff; under parts of body white; bill and legs black. Female, upper parts brown instead of black.

NEST: Made of fine grasses, moss and hair; situated on the ground beneath a clod of earth or in a heap of stones, or in a crevice in a stone wall.

EGGS: 5 to 7 in number; pale greenish-blue, often delicately and faintly spotted with brown. (Plate 8, fig. 6a).

DIPPER (*Cinclus aquaticus*).

(Plate 9, fig. 5).

This bird is rarely seen in the south but is by no means uncommon in the northern counties and quite plentiful in Scotland and Ireland. It is about the size of a Thrush but differs greatly in appearance being somewhat like a large Wren in shape and movements. The most likely place in which the Dipper may be seen is on a boulder or fallen tree trunk rising out of the water. From such a position the bird can dip, or dive, beneath the surface and return to its original vantage point. It is local in distribution often inhabiting the same spot year after year.

The plumage is of contrasting colours; the head, wings and back are very dark brown, while the throat, breast and

under parts are white. The colouring of the female is less
sharply defined, the brown is more of a grey-brown and the
under parts a dirty white.

NEST: Composed of leaves and moss, lined with feathers
and usually well hidden in a crevice in a rock or in a hole in
a bank.

EGGS: 4 to 6 in number; pure white, somewhat pointed
at one end. (Plate 9, fig. 5a).

SWIFT (*Cypselus apus*).
(Plate 9, fig. 3).

The Swift is a common summer visitor but a late arrival,
sometimes making its appearance several weeks after the
Swallow and Martins have reached these shores. One of the
chief distinguishing features between this bird and the
Swallow is its extraordinary endurance of flight, for it is
seldom seen perching, like the Swallow, but spends most of
its time from dawn till dusk whirling through the air in search
of food which consists entirely of small winged insects. The
wing expanse is very considerable in proportion to the size
of the body.

The darker parts of the plumage are jet black and the
surest means of distinguishing it from the Swallow, when
seen close to, is the grey patch on the throat. The female is
slightly smaller and the plumage is of a dark, rusty brown.

Just before dusk these birds often ascend to a great height
and, in large numbers, whirl round and round the sky
uttering a shrill, squeaking noise and darting up and down
with remarkable rapidity.

As the Swift is a late arrival and, curiously enough one of
the earliest to leave the country in the autumn, the nesting
operations commence immediately on its arrival; it is, therefore engaged in nest building and rearing its young practically
the whole of its time while in this part of the world.

NEST: Unlike the plastered, mud structure of the Swallow,
the nest of the Swift is made of coarse grass and dead leaves,

PLATE 9.

1. House Martin.
2. Swallow.
3. Swift.
4. Sand Martin.
5. Dipper.

1a. Egg.
2a. Egg.
3a. Egg.
4a. Egg.
5a. Egg.

cemented together with saliva and lined with feathers. It is crudely made and of no particular design. When near habitation it is usually situated in an out-house or under a roof, but in wilder districts a crevice in a rock or other such position is selected.

EGGS: 2 in number; pure white; somewhat elongated. (Plate 9, fig. 3a).

SWALLOW (*Hirundo rustica*).
(Plate 9, fig. 2).

A much more familiar bird than the Swift and more often observed at close quarters owing to its habit of perching on housetops, telegraph wires and other such places. It does not spend anything like so much time on the wing as the Swift. The names Chimney Swallow and House Swallow accurately describe the bird because of the habit it possesses of frequenting dwelling-houses. It is the first of its kind to arrive in this country from its winter quarters in Africa, being seen early in April in favourable seasons, but nesting does not, as a rule, begin before early May. It is an insect eater, catching its prey while on the wing and flying and swooping low over ponds and meadows.

Not much difficulty need be experienced in identifying this species from the Swift, the chief distinguishing feature, apart from the colouring of the plumage, is the very long, forked tail. The back, wings and top of the head are dark blue; the under parts whitish, tinged with red; breast and throat of the male chestnut brown, while in the female the breast is less reddish and the under parts pure white.

NEST: Constructed of mud in which are a few pieces of grass, profusely lined with feathers. Most often placed under the eaves of a house, or fastened against a wall of an out-house or farm-building.

EGGS: 4 to 6 in number; white, delicately speckled with brown at the larger end. There are two or three broods during the season, sometimes more. (Plate 9, fig. 2a).

HOUSE MARTIN (*Hirundo urbica*).
(Plate 9, fig. 1).

This bird closely resembles the Swallow in habits but is at once distinguished by the plumage. It haunts dwelling-houses and farm-buildings, and is sometimes known as the Window Swallow. It arrives soon after the Swallow and is usually seen in the same surroundings as the latter bird. The best means of distinguishing the House Martin from the Swallow or Swift is by the much slower and steadier flight, for it does not twist or turn about in the air as is the case with the other two species, but proceeds in a graceful gliding motion. In wilder districts away from habitation this Martin is usually observed in colonies near water where the insect food is plentiful and where cliffs and steep banks afford suitable sites.

The plumage above is blue-black and the breast and under parts pure white; the tail less forked than that of the Swallow, and much shorter.

NEST: Made of mud and lined with feathers and with a small entrance hole towards the top. In towns it is situated under the eaves of a house or not uncommly against a wall.

EGGS: 4 to 5 in number; pure white. (Plate 9, fig. 1a).

SAND MARTIN (*Hirundo riparia*).
(Plate 9, fig. 4).

Although found almost everywhere in the neighbourhood of water, and especially near sand-pits, this Martin is, perhaps, most abundantly seen on the coast, the most favourite haunts being cliffs in which it can build its nest. It is the smallest of the Swallow family and one of the earliest arrivals, usually making its appearance during the first weeks of April. It often congregates in colonies and is seldom seen singly. In appearance it is not unlike the House Martin but smaller, and the upper parts dark brown instead of blue; breast and under parts white.

The food consists of insects obtained while on the wing but these birds do not remain in the air for any great length of time but frequently return to the face of the cliff to which they cling, and rest awhile before again taking to the wing.

NEST: Composed of grass, well lined with feathers. The nest is situated at the end of a tunnel, two-and-a-half to three feet long which is made in the face of a cliff or sandpit.

EGGS: 4 to 6 in number; pure white, like those of the House Martin, but more pointed. (Plate 9, fig. 4a).

KINGFISHER (*Alcedo ispido*).
(Plate 10, fig. 4).

The gorgeous plumage of the Kingfisher allows it to rank as one of the most beautiful of British birds. It is always found in the vicinity of water, especially streams, as it feeds on small fish; the method by which it catches its prey, by skimming over the surface of the water and suddenly darting on a fish which has ventured too near the surface, enables its identity to be established if observed while so engaged.

The only note uttered is a piercing cry usually heard when the bird is on the wing.

The back is blue, the head and wings being of a more greenish-blue and the throat white. There is a red band beneath the eye and below this is a band of green; under parts orange; legs and feet red. The bill is very stout, black but orange at the base.

NEST: Composed mostly of fish-bones; situated at the end of a hole in the bank of a stream.

EGGS: 6 to 8 in number; pure glossy-white, rounded at both ends. (Plate 10, fig. 4a).

GREEN WOODPECKER (*Picus viridis*).
(Plate 10, fig. 1).

This is the largest of the British Woodpeckers and well distributed throughout the country.

The variety of colours which go to make up the glorious plumage of this bird make it, without doubt, the handsomest

of any creature found in the woods. The head and back are olive-green and the under parts pale green; the face is black and the top of the head crimson; bill long and tail sturdy. Most often seen clinging to the trunk of a tree, the claws of the bird being so made as to allow it to move around the tree with remarkable agility.

Although various fruits and seeds constitute part of its diet, the chief food of this Woodpecker consists of insects and, with the aid of its strong bill it hunts for these in the bark; the loud tapping sound so familiarly heard in the woods is caused by the bird hunting for insects or building its nesting-hole.

NEST: A mass of wood-chips at the bottom of a hole in a tree; the opening just large enough for the bird to enter.

EGGS: 5 to 7 in number, glossy white. (Plate 10, fig. 1a).

LESSER SPOTTED WOODPECKER
(*Dendrocopus minor*).
(Plate 10, fig. 5).

This bird resembles the Great Spotted Woodpecker in habits but is four inches smaller and the markings are in the form of bars rather than spots which is the reason for the alternative, and perhaps, more appropriate name of Barred Woodpecker. It is seldom, if ever, seen on the ground but, like the other members of the Woodpecker family, feeds on insects in the bark of trees. Its characteristic habit of tapping the bark with its strong bill, in search of food, can be heard at a considerable distance.

The upper parts of this bird are black, spotted and barred with white except the centre tail feathers which are black without any markings; the face is white, the crown crimson; wings black, barred with white; under parts of body white. Female similar but lacks the crimson crown.

NEST: A hole in a tree trunk at the end of which is a cavity well lined with wood-chips.

EGGS: 6 to 7 in number; pure white, roundish. (Plate 10, fig. 5a).

CUCKOO (*Cuculus canorus*).

(Plate 10, fig. 2).

The Cuckoo possesses such distinct peculiarities as to render it immediately distinguishable from other British summer visitors. Its song, or call note, is very distinctive as well as its mode of flight, and the fact that it builds no nest of its own but deposits its eggs in the nests of other birds, makes it an interesting creature. The song is totally unlike that of any other bird in these Isles and requires no description and the irregular, clumsy flight, showing clearly the long tail, identifies it at once when observed on the wing.

Its food consists chiefly of insects, especially grubs; it possesses a particular liking for hairy caterpillars.

The plumage on the upper parts is bluish-grey; the under parts whitish; the breast is streaked with darker markings on a bluish-grey background; the tail, which is a very dark grey, has several white markings.

Its visit to this country is not of long duration for it leaves in late summer, in fact it is one of the first migratory birds to return to warmer regions.

The nests of those birds in which the Cuckoo deposits its eggs are the Hedge Sparrow, Robin, Tree Pipit, Meadow Pipit as well as several others. Only one egg is placed in each nest, the colouring of the eggs vary considerably, usually being somewhat similar to those of the bird which is to become the foster-mother. (Plate 10, fig. 2a).

WRYNECK (*Iynx torquilla*).

(Plate 10, fig. 3).

Arriving in April this bird is almost entirely confined to the south-eastern counties of England and it is rare or even absent in the Midlands and northwards. Having a particular liking for ants among its varied insect diet it is often seen on the ground in the vicinity of ant hills and sometimes may be observed c.inging to the trunk of a tree hunting for these insects in the bark. Its name is derived from the characteristic manner in which it moves its flexible neck while so engaged in

58

searching the bark of trees and this characteristic affords a good means of identifying the bird. In many ways the Wryneck resembles the Woodpecker, even to nesting in a hole in a tree but does not tap the bark like the last-named birds.

The upper parts are brownish-grey, speckled with dark brown, black and buff; head and throat pale buff with darker cross bands; under parts white.

NEST: A hole in a tree trunk, usually in decaying wood; the nest itself is composed of fragments of rotten wood.

EGGS: 7 to 9 in number; pure white. (Plate 10, fig. 3a).

BARN OWL (*Strix flammea*).
(Plate 11, fig. 4).

Those who have witnessed this fine Owl on the wing, may rightly consider it to be a White Owl, for it is the only Owl in this country with a large proportion of white in its plumage. Strictly it is not white in the same manner as the Snowy Owl of the northern regions which is white all over, for the Barn Owl is only white on the under parts of the body and the under sides of the wings and tail, thus giving the bird a whitish appearance when seen from beneath. The upper parts are pale brown with a golden tinge, mottled with grey, and richly speckled with black.

As the name suggests this Owl is fond of sleeping in barns and out-houses and will usually choose such places when possible in preference to trees. Other favourite sleeping quarters chosen by this nocturnal species in which to spend the daytime in seclusion are church towers, cavities in walls and old buildings and cliffs and similar dark places. It emerges at twilight flying with quick strokes and proceeding noiselessly in search of its prey which consists of mice, rats, shrews and other small rodents.

The cry is harsh and consists of a rasping screech.

NEST: No nest is built at all, the eggs being laid in dark, well secluded corners of barns, cliffs and similar situations.

EGGS: 2 in number; pure white, rounded at both ends. A pair of eggs is laid successively. (Plate 11, fig. 4a).

PLATE 11.

1. Short-eared Owl.   1a. Egg.
2. Long-eared Owl.   2a. Egg.
3. Tawny Owl.   3a. Egg.
4. Barn Owl.   4a. Egg.

LONG-EARED OWL (*Asio otus*).

(Plate 11, fig. 2).

One of the most widely distributed of our native Owls, being found in wooded districts throughout the British Isles. Unlike the Barn Owl this bird does not inhabit barns and church towers but must be sought in its favourite haunts in pine woods where it spends the daytime asleep on a branch close to the trunk of the tree where it harmonises so closely with its surroundings as to deceive not only human eyes but the eyes of small birds that flit past this bird of prey apparently unaware of its presence. Although the same length as the Barn Owl the Long-Eared Owl is very much slimmer in build and this slim form together with the long head-tufts will always distinguish it from the other Owls.

The diet is purely carnivorous, rats, mice and similar small creatures, comprising its food.

The colouring of the upper parts is buff, finely spotted with brown and grey and with dark brown streaks; the buff wing and tail feathers have distinct dark brown cross-bars; under parts of body generally buff with dark brown cross-bars and numerous streaks of the same colour; legs and feet feathered.

NEST: This bird builds no nest of its own but lays its eggs in the old deserted nests of Rooks, Crows and Magpies.

EGGS: 4 to 6 in number; pure white, rounded. (Plate 11, fig. 2a).

TAWNY OWL (*Syrnium aluco*).

(Plate 11, fig. 3).

This owl is found in nearly all wooded districts of England and Wales and in the south of Scotland where it may be readily identified by its familiar utterance " Too-whit." The day-time is spent in trees but unlike the Long-Eared Owl, this bird always conceals itself in holes in trees, and only very occasionally is it met with sitting on a branch close against the trunk. It may often be observed in the early evening flying slowly over the low-growing herbage on the edge of a wood in search of mice, shrews and other small nocturnal mammals.

In general colouring this bird very much resembles the Long-Eared Owl but is more plump in form. Ruddy-brown is the predominant colour of the upper parts, this being mottled with grey and dark brown, and whitish on the nape; the wings have two rows of largish white spots; under parts pale buff, spotted with brown and streaked with dark brown; legs and feet covered with white feathers.

NEST: No nest is built, the eggs being deposited in the old nest of a Magpie or Rook, or in a hole in a hollow tree.

EGGS: 3 to 4 in number; plain white, rounded. (Plate 11, fig. 3a).

SHORT-EARED OWL (*Asio crachyotus*).

(Plate 11, fig. 1).

Closely resembling the Long-Eared Owl in general form but without the long head-tufts of the latter bird; the colouring, too, is similar, only differing in detail, the chief characteristic markings being the grey face and a ring of black feathers encircling the yellow eyes. The upper parts are tawny in colouring, heavily streaked with dark brown; under parts lighter buff and unstreaked; dark brown cross-bars on the larger wing-feathers. The chief feature which distinguishes this bird from the other Owls is the small head in comparison to the rest of the body.

It is much less common in the South of England than the Barn, Tawny or Long-Eared Owls, being found most plentifully in the north of England and in Scotland, and is usually known in the south as a winter migrant. Another interesting point about this bird is its apparent dislike for trees, for it is nearly always found on, or near, the ground; it flies at dusk over the open country in search of its prey. It also has the habit of feeding by day as well as at night. The cry is very varied ranging from a high-pitched hissing noise to a low, hollow baying hoot.

NEST: On the ground, being a mere depression among tufts of grass and heather.

EGGS: 6 to 8 in number; pure white, rounded. (Plate 11, fig. 1a).

PEREGRIN FALCON (*Falco peregrinus*).
(Plate 12, fig. 5).

This fine Falcon is confined chiefly to the coasts, but inland cliffs and rocky mountainous districts especially in Scotland also provide good breeding sites. It may be found almost anywhere around the coasts of England but is most common in the northern half of the country and especially in Scotland and Ireland.

For its size it is a particularly fierce bird of prey, attacking large birds such as partridges, grouse, ducks and pigeons; it possesses a very direct method of attack, flying swiftly and swooping with great speed on its victim. When alarmed, or disturbed during the nesting season it utters a loud, harsh cry, " Hek, Hek, Hek."

The upper parts of the plumage are dark bluish-grey; the head and neck blackish; a patch of pure white appears on the throat and sides of the neck; under parts of the body white with distinct, fine dark brown cross-bars; the white also prevails on the under sides of the wings and tail; legs and feet yellow. The female is more generally brown instead of the bluish-grey of the male.

NEST: Very little attempt is made at nest building, the eggs being placed on the ledge of a cliff when on the coast, or when breeding inland in holes and crevices in church towers and sometimes in the old nests of Crows.

EGGS: 2 to 4 in number; ground colour pale buff, but the dark reddish-brown markings are so profuse as to practically cover the egg, so that only here and there is a patch of the paler ground-colouring visible. (Plate 12, fig. 5a).

HOBBY (*Falco subbuteo*).
(Plate 12, fig. 2).

At one time not uncommon, the Hobby has now become a rare bird in this country and is confined almost entirely to the southern half of England, being exceedingly scarce further north and almost absent in Scotland, and quite absent in Ireland. True to its kind the Hobby is a bird of prey but

PLATE 12.

1.	Sparrow Hawk.	1a.	Egg.
2.	Hobby.	2a.	Egg.
3.	Merlin.	3a.	Egg.
4.	Kestrel.	4a.	Egg.
5.	Peregrin Falcon.	5a.	Egg.

it also feeds extensively on insects of the larger varieties such as dragon-flies, cockchafers and other large beetles of the cockchafer variety usually catching them while on the wing. It is known for its remarkably rapid flight, the long, pointed wings enabling it to strike down small birds as they fly over the open country, not too far from woods, where it returns with its prey. It is essentially a tree bird resorting to the woods when not engaged in hunting for food; the nest is always placed in the upper branches of a tree.

The colouring of the upper part is slate-grey, becoming paler towards the tail, and, like the Peregrin Falcon, the throat and sides of the neck are pure white; breast and under parts of body white with longitudinal streaks of dark brown; under sides of wings and tail white, with black bars. Female similar in markings but generally duller in colouring.

NEST: No individual nest is constructed, the old nest of a Wood Pigeon, Magpie or Crow being selected with a few additions made by the Hobby itself.

EGGS: 3 to 5 in number; ground colouring pale buff, densely mottled with reddish-brown. (Plate 12, fig. 2a).

MERLIN (*Falco aesalon*).
(Plate 12, fig. 3).

The smallest of the British Hawks and more or less generally distributed in the lowlands during the winter months, but in the breeding season the Southern districts of England are forsaken for the mountainous regions of Northen England, Scotland, Ireland and Wales. Not all the Merlins are resident birds, some leaving these shores in the autumn for warmer climes and at such seasons of departure they are often seen by the sea-shore. The Merlin is a bird of prey living almost entirely on small birds which it swoops upon while on the wing with great pertinacity.

The plumage on the back is slate-blue ; the head the same colour but with black collar just below the nape; the largest of the wing-feathers black; under parts of body blue-grey; under sides of wings white with dark brown bars; legs and feet yellow.

NEST: Little more than a hollow among heather or on moorland; sometimes a small amount of dry heather is used as lining.

EGGS: 4 to 6 in number; buff, very densely mottled with reddish-brown. (Plate 12, fig. 3a).

KESTREL HAWK (*Falco tinnunculus*).
(Plate 12, fig. 4).

This bird is the commonest of the Hawks found in Britain and certainly the most likely to be seen in the countryside. It is larger than the Sparrow Hawk.

The plumage is of sombre hue and there are few distinctive markings to afford immediate identification except when observed at close quarters. The bird is, therefore, best distinguished when on the wing and it is while so engaged that it is usually seen. The chief characteristic feature is its peculiar habit of hovering in mid-air while searching for its prey. The Kestrel often hovers at a great height, and the wings vibrate with so little motion that the bird appears to be motionless in the air. It has the habit of swooping suddenly and then hovering again in a different place. It is able to maintain itself in the air in this fashion for a remarkably long period.

The back and head are dark grey; wings brownish grey, streaked with reddish-brown; under sides similar to back but of a paler tint. The female is lighter in colour.

The food consists mainly of mice, rats, small birds and certain insects. The cry is a short series of shrill utterances, somewhat roughly interpreted as " ry, ry, ry."

NEST: Usually on a ledge of cliff or in cavities in old quarries. Sometimes the old nest of a Magpie or Crow is used.

EGGS: 4 to 6 in number; buffish-white, very densely mottled with reddish-brown. (Plate 12, fig. 4a).

SPARROW HAWK (*Falco nisus*).
(Plate 12, fig. 1).

Not so plentiful as the Kestrel Hawk but fairly common

all over the country, being found mostly in the wildest parts, especially on common land and wastes with woods not far distant, where it may return to a safe retreat when not hunting for food.

Like other members of this family it is a bird of prey, obtaining its food by hovering over the most likely spot, for mice and small birds, by beating the air with its wings, then making a sudden swoop to the ground and pouncing on its unsuspecting victim.

The male bird has bluish-grey wings, head and back, and is whitish beneath, tinged with red. The head and back in the female are brown.

NEST: Sometimes the nest of a Crow is used but more often the nest is placed in a tree in a wood and composed of twigs and is lossely constructed. It nests late for a resident bird, May being the usual month and occasionally not until June.

EGGS: 4 to 6 in number; bluish-white, densely blotched with reddish-brown, mostly at the larger end. (Plate 12, fig. 1a).

MALLARD (*Anas boschas*).
(Plate 13, fig. 4.)

Mallard is the name given to the male of the species of Duck known as the Wild Duck. These birds are the commonest and most often seen of any of the Duck family which inhabit these Islands and they may be found well distributed all over the country. Being very strong of wing they sometimes fly at a great height, making extraordinary rapid progress as they head in a very definite direction and the distinctive feature while in the air is the long neck craned forward. They sometimes appear in the sky in considerable numbers but always proceeding in orderly formation.

The food consists of all manner of small insects and various aquatic animal life found at the bottom of a pond or lake, as well as in mud-flats and on marshland. The familiar flat, shovel-like bill is well adapted for obtaining their food in such places and is characteristic of this species of bird.

The male is a particularly beautiful creature adorned in

PLATE 13.

1.	Pochard.	1a.	Egg.
2.	Eider Duck.	2a.	Egg.
3.	Teal.	3a.	Egg.
4.	Mallard.	4a.	Egg.

very gaily coloured plumage. The head and neck are wonderfully marked with green and with a white collar round the latter; the breast a rich reddish-brown; the under parts whitish. Four of the tail feathers are curled upwards and these are white in colour; legs and webbed-feet bright orange. The female lacks these contrasting colours and is a mottled brown all over.

NEST: Constructed of coarse grass and reeds; always situated near water and usually placed among the rushes.

EGGS: 10 to 12 in number; pale grey-green. (Plate 13, fig. 4a).

EIDER DUCK (*Somateria mollissima*).
(Plate 13, fig. 2).

The breeding-grounds of this Duck extend from the North of Scotland to the Farne Islands as well as on some of the many small islands of the West coast of Scotland. During the winter months, however, many of the birds migrate southwards and the Eider Duck is, therefore, only known as a winter visitor around the southern coasts of England. It is strictly a sea bird and never found inland as it is dependent for its food on diving for crabs and shellfish in salt water. Even on the coast it is seldom observed on land for its spends the daytime out at sea, only returning to the rocky coasts at nightfall. Eider Ducks are rarely seen singly, but in numbers keeping close together when diving for food. Except in the breeding season, when it utters an indistinct cooing sound it is a silent bird.

The upper parts of the body are white; crown of the head black but face and throat white and nape pale green; bill olive-green; wings and tail black; under parts black; legs and feet olive green. Female generally brown, lighter brown beneath. The name is derived from the well-known eider-down.

NEST: Composed of grass and seaweed, lined with down; situated on the ground near the water's edge.

EGGS: 5 to 7 in number; green. (Plate 13, fig. 2a).

POCHARD (*Fuligula ferina*).
(Plate 13, fig. 1).

The Pochard is found much more plentifully on inland waters than around the coast although it is not uncommon in the latter districts. Being a resident it may be observed all the year round, but during the winter months its numbers are greatly increased by winter migrants and during this season is often a familiar sight on large ponds and lakes inland. Being an expert diver it obtains its food in the form of aquatic insects and animals at the bottom of the pond and also swims with great ease and rapidity with its body sunk low in the water, and its neck drawn well in. It is principally a night-feeder but may also be seen during the day on frequent occasions. Vegetable food composes a certain portion of its diet but worms and grubs are most sought after.

The characteristic feature of the Pochard is the chestnut coloured head and neck; the back and upper parts of the breast black; tail dark brown; wings greyish-brown; under parts of body white with fine cross-bars of black; legs and feet blue-grey.

NEST: Situated among rushes or other herbage at the water's edge and lined with feathers from the bird's breast.

EGGS: 7 to 12 in number; greenish. (Plate 13, fig. 1a).

TEAL (*Querquedula crecca*).
(Plate 13, fig. 3).

This is the smallest of our British Ducks and is generally distributed throughout the British Isles, breeding near inland waters and feeding in ponds, lakes and on marshy ground, its food consisting chiefly of worms and slugs as well as aquatic plants. Being a night-feeder it is not so likely to be seen during the daytime except when disturbed while resting among the rushes or low herbage near the water's edge. It usually occurs in flocks and does not associate much with other species of Ducks. During the winter its numbers are greatly increased by winter migrants. The call note is an abrupt " crick."

In general appearance it is a squat, plump bird with a variety of colouring in the plumage. The bill is black; the head and neck chestnut-brown with a green band curving from the eye to the nape of the neck, this being edged with a yellow line; back mottled with dark grey; wings grey; breast buff with numerous dark brown spots; under parts of body whitish; feet and legs dusky. Female dark brown above instead of chestnut-brown.

NEST: Composed of grasses and leaves and lined with feathers from the bird's breast; situated on the ground, usually under cover of a bush by the water's edge.

EGGS: 8 to 10 in number; pale green or greenish-buff. (Plate 13, fig. 3a).

CORMORANT (*Plalacrocorax carbo*).
(Plate 14, fig. 5).

One of the most interesting of British sea-birds and fairly common around the coast. It is a familiar sight when swimming in the sea, often in rough weather, and continually diving beneath the surface in search of fish which constitute its food. From a distance it need never be confused with other sea-birds owing to the manner in which it sits very low in the water and, when sighted from the shore, the neck alone appears to be above water. When not engaged in feeding it sits on some prominent piece of rock, or jutting ledge often remaining motionless for long periods. The call note is a harsh cry like a broken croak.

The plumage is black with the exception of the white throat and thigh and the characteristic feature is the crest on the head. The female is larger than the male and the colouring of the plumage is very dull black.

NEST: A bulky structure composed of sticks, dry grass and seaweed. Cormorants usually nest in colonies on cliffs overlooking the sea and only very occasionally inland, in which case the nest is situated in a bush and more rarely in a tree.

EGGS : 3 to 5 in number; chalky-white, surface rough. (Plate 14, fig. 5a).

PLATE 14.

1.	Shag.	1a.	Egg.
2.	Golden Plover.	2a.	Egg.
3.	Oyster Catcher.	3a.	Egg.
4.	Gannet.	4a.	Egg.
5.	Cormorant.	5a.	Egg.

SHAG (*Cormoran largup*).
(Plate 14, fig. 1).

The Shag is the popular name for the Green Cormorant which is a much smaller bird than the Cormorant, but somewhat resembles it in appearance and habits and is less abundant. It is a shore-loving bird and local in distribution, being found sparsely in some districts while in other localities it is seen in great numbers on the rocks and cliffs, more especially around the east coast and in Scotland.

The cry is harsh and not so loud as its near relative the Cormorant. It has similar habits of diving for fish, which it performs with remarkable agility.

Dark green is the predominant colouring of the head, back and under parts of the body, but the wings and tail are black; the whitish patch on the thigh, as in the Cormorant, is less distinct and totally absent during the breeding season; the crest on the head is less significant.

NEST: Similar to that of the Cormorant.

EGGS: 3 to 4 in number; similar to those of Cormorant, but smaller. (Plate 14, fig. 1a).

GANNET (*Sula Cassana*).
(Plate 14, fig. 4).

This bird is rarely seen except on the coast and is exceedingly local in distribution. In Scotland and Ireland it is often observed on the rocky coasts in numbers while in other localities it is scarce, or absent. The most favoured haunts are the remote rocky islands off the coasts of the northern parts of Scotland where it is often abundant. The cry is very harsh.

Gannets feed largely on fish which they obtain by diving beneath the surface. They first soar into the air to watch for their prey and then swoop downwards, similar to the habits of a hawk.

The plumage is white with the exception of the head and neck which are pale brown, and the tips of the wings which are black; the bill is large and a prominent feature of the bird.

Nest: Made of grass and seaweed. These birds breed in large colonies on the rocks and the nests are placed on a ledge.

Eggs: 1 only ; chalk-white. (Plate 14, fig 4a).

OYSTER-CATCHER (*Haematopus ostrabegus*).
(Plate 14, fig. 3).

A typical shore bird more plentiful in the north of England and in Scotland, but may be seen anywhere around the coasts of the British Isles. It will always attract attention by its loud shrill cry and, when not feeding will most often be seen perched on a piece of rock or ledge of cliff facing the sea, and is a real sentinel of the more unfrequented and wild stretches of coast.

The Oyster-Catcher is so named owing to its reputed liking for oysters, but it is doubtful if such shellfish constitute a large portion of the diet, in fact many authorities assert their disbelief that the oyster is eaten by this bird at all, it feeding largely on mussels and small shellfish and various marine creatures such as crabs.

The very distinct markings of this bird will provide no difficulty in identifying it for it possesses a contrasting black and white plumage. The head, throat, back and wings are jet black and the rest of the body white; the legs are dark flesh-colour and the bill bright orange.

Nest: Usually situated on the ground among shingle and composed of small pebbles and fragments of shell.

Eggs: 3 in number; pale buff, spotted and streaked with dark brown and grey. (Plate 14, fig. 3a).

GOLDEN PLOVER (*Charadrius pluvialis*).
(Plate 14, fig. 2).

This handsome bird is a migrant within the country, that is to say, it breeds in the north and migrates south during the winter. Although found plentifully on moorlands and heaths inland during the summer, such places are forsaken during the winter when the severe weather makes it necessary for it to move to the coast in order to obtain its food more easily. Newly planted cornfields and ploughed land on the coast are the most likely neighbourhoods to observe this Plover in the winter.

They often move about in flocks, and numbers may be seen to rise suddenly if disturbed while feeding, uttering a shrill cry, and whirling round and round before settling again.

The plumage varies considerably in the summer and winter but the name Golden Plover is particularly descriptive of this bird when seen in the breeding season. The upper parts are very deep grey, profusely marked with yellow or golden streaks; the head has a distinct white line above the eye and on each side of the neck; head, breast and under parts black. In winter lightish brown takes the place of the black.

NEST: Merely a depression in the ground usually situated among heather or even on the bare earth and sometimes scantily lined with heather.

EGGS: 4 in number; pale stone colour, richly blotched with dark brown. (Plate 14, fig. 2a).

WOOD PIGEON (*Columba palumbus*).
(Plate 15, fig. 1).

Also known as the Ring-Dove on account of the whitish feathers which almost encircle the neck. This is the British wild Pigeon and the most familiar, being well distributed throughout the country. As the name implies, the favourite haunt of this bird is the woods but it is also fond of inhabiting solitary trees where the trunk is covered with ivy. The note is a soft " coo-o, coo-o."

The colouring of the head and neck is bluish-grey and the tail feathers black; the breast is of a lighter tint and with various greenish and reddish tinges, while the whole plumage

PLATE 15.

1. Wood Pigeon.
2. Stock Dove.
3. Turtle Dove.
4. Little Grebe.
5. Red-Throated Diver.

1a. Egg.
2a. Egg.
3a. Egg.
4a. Egg.
5a. Egg.

has a distinct purplish reflection; bill orange; feet and legs red.

NEST: Made of twigs and coarse roots and situated in a variety of places such as holes in trees, in ivy around the trunk as well as in caverns in cliffs, and even in rabbit holes.

EGGS: 2 in number; pure glossy-white, roundish. (Plate 15, fig. 2a).

TURTLE DOVE (*Turtur communis*).
(Plate 15, fig. 3).

Not so widely distributed as the other British Doves for, being a migratory species its breeding localities are confined to the south of England, becoming more scarce in Yorkshire and practically unknown in Scotland, Ireland or Wales. It arrives on these shores in late April and haunts woods. Its arrival may be known by its continually uttered " coo-rrr."

As compared with the other members of this family of birds it is of slight build and flies swiftly, often at a great height, especially when observed flying over the open country.

The head, nape and back are greyish-red, the back distinctly ruddy; wings greyish, the principal feathers darker grey; breast reddish; under parts white; feet and legs red.

NEST: Usually built entirely of twigs, very slightly constructed and fragile and placed in the branch of a tree.

EGGS: 2 in number; creamy-white, roundish. (Plate 15, fig. 3a).

LITTLE GREBE (*Tachybaptes fluviatilis*).
(Plate 15, fig. 4).

This bird is fairly general in distribution being found most plentifully in the south, but by no means scarce in the northern districts. A typical water bird, the Little Grebe or Dabchick, may be found on marshland, around ponds and lakes, and on the banks of rivers and streams. In general appearance it somewhat resembles a duck, but the pointed bill and small size of the bird will always distinguish it from the Ducks, likewise it need never be confused with the Moorhen or Coot, both these birds being nearly twice the size. It is particularly shy and must be approached with silent step for at the least sign of danger it will take to the water and, swimming with great speed, cross the pond and disappear into the low-growing herbage on the opposite side.

The head is blackish, while the cheeks are chestnut-brown; back dark brown; under parts white; the bill is black, tipped with white; feet and legs blackish-green.

NEST: Composed of a quantity of aquatic plants often floating on the water or sometimes in the herbage at the water's edge.

EGGS: 4 to 6 in number ; creamy-white. (Plate 15, fig. 4a).

RED-THROATED DIVER (*Colymbus septentrionalis*).

(Plate 15, fig. 5).

Those birds seen around the coast of England in winter are migrants from the more northerly parts of Scotland, where the Red-Throated Diver breeds.

Owing to the peculiar formation of the feet, together with the fact that the legs are set far back, it has difficulty in walking on land and can only proceed with a slow waddle, and for this reason it keeps mostly to the water. As the name implies, it is an expert diver and when alarmed will disappear beneath the surface reappearing some considerable distance away. The food is composed almost entirely of fish which is obtained by diving, the bird being able to remain beneath the water for a remarkably long time. When not so engaged it sits on the surface with the body deep in the water and the long neck, characteristic of the Divers, drawn in between the shoulders, which gives it the appearance of a duck.

The upper parts of the plumage are dark brown, streaked with black and white, while the sides of the neck are grey; throat bright red, from which the bird takes its name; under parts white.

NEST: Untidy structure of seaweed, placed not far from the water's edge.

EGGS: 2 in number; ground colouring darkish-brown with darker reddish-brown blotches. (Plate 15, fig. 5a).

LAPWING (*Vanellus cristatus*).
(Plate 16, fig. 4).

This species is generally distributed, being found inland in great numbers as well as on the coast. The Lapwing is the commonest and most familiar member of the Plover family and is also known as the Peewit or Green Plover. The well-known cry " Pee-wit " is uttered repeatedly when the birds are disturbed while feeding in meadows or on ploughed land and especially while nesting, and this cry being peculiar to the species will always assist in identification. During the winter these birds move about in large colonies breaking up into smaller companies during the breeding season.

The Lapwing is easily recognized when seen at fairly close quarters by the characteristic crest, most prominent in the male. Green is the general colouring of the upper parts of the body; throat, cheeks and upper part of breast greenish-black; sides of face and neck white; wing-feathers black; tail white, with broad black band towards the end; under parts of body white. The tail is rounded and somewhat broad.

NEST: Built in a slight hollow in the ground; only a small amount of nesting material is used.

EGGS: 4 in number; olive-brown or olive-green, blotched and spotted with dark brown and grey. (Plate 16, fig. 4a).

SANDPIPER (*Tringa hypoleueos*).
(Plate 16, fig. 1).

Fairly well distributed throughout the country but generally more abundant in the north and particularly in Scotland. It is to be met with in the neighbourhood of streams, large ponds, lakes and riverside inland as well as near the coast.

PLATE 16.

1.	Sandpiper.	1a.	Egg.
2.	Redshank.	2a.	Egg.
3.	Snipe	3a.	Egg.
4.	Lapwing.	4a.	Egg.

It is, to a certain extent local, being found much more plentifully in some districts than in others.

The sandpiper can hardly be said to possess a song but in the breeding season the male utters an attractive cry, certainly musical in tone. The food consists almost entirely of insects and grubs.

The back, wings and tail are grey-brown, with a tinge of olive; head also grey-brown but with a patch of white on the sides of the neck; the breast is of a lighter hue and streaked with greyish-white; under parts white.

NEST: Composed of dry grass and moss, placed on the ground, under cover of a large tuft of grass, usually near water.

EGGS: 4 in number; pear-shaped, creamy-white or pale yellow, blotched with reddish-brown. (Plate 16, fig. 1a).

REDSHANK (*Tringa totanus*).

(Plate 16, fig. 2).

An inhabitant of the sea-shore and marshlands but most usually found on the East Coast. It is by no means a common bird and one of the least abundant of the Plover family. Its food is composed chiefly of insects, grubs and small crabs, the latter being obtained on the sand-flats when the tide is out. Inland the Redshank is seldom seen, but river estuaries and salt-flats are favourite haunts, especially the more secluded localities. The cry is clear and loud and can only be described as somewhat resembling a piercing scream, especially when disturbed while feeding.

The head, back and wings are pale brown, profusely streaked with darker brown; under parts of body white; tail-feathers white, streaked and barred with black; legs and feet bright orange. In winter the under parts become more grey than brown and the general colouring of the plumage of both sexes is more sombre.

The breeding grounds are usually situated on marshlands, which are well covered with large tufts of grass in which the nests are placed. The nests are well concealed and very difficult to detect unless the bird is aroused while sitting and so revealing the whereabouts of the nest.

NEST: Not elaborate in structure but carefully made of dry grass and moss.

EGGS: 4 in number; pale buff, spotted and blotched with reddish-brown and grey. (Plate 16, fig. 2a).

SNIPE (*Gallinago coelestris*).
(Plate 16, fig. 3).

Common and well distributed throughout the British Isles; a resident bird but its numbers are greatly increased during the winter by migratory birds. Being of an extremely shy nature it is far less in evidence than the other species of birds belonging to this family and often haunts marshlands and undergrowth near woods, but keeping mostly to the open country, where it remains well hidden in low-growing herbage. As its food consists of worms and grubs it feeds by probing the mud with its long bill and when so engaged almost squats on the ground, its colouring harmonizing so closely with its surroundings as to render it extremely difficult to see. When approached it springs up into the air almost at one's feet. The cry is loud and startling, especially when uttered when the bird rises from the ground close at hand.

The bill is very long and thin, straight and brown in colouring. Upper parts of body white, heavily barred with brown; head white, crown barred lengthwise with buff and dark brown; neck and breast streaked with brown; under parts white, barred with brown on the flanks; legs olive-green.

NEST: A depression in the ground, scantily lined with dry pieces of herbage.

EGGS: 4 in number; greenish-white, densely blotched with reddish and purplish-brown at the larger end in the shape of a cone. (Plate 16, fig. 3a).

WOODCOCK (*Scolopax rusticola*).
(Plate 17, fig. 1).

A favourite game-bird closely allied to the Snipe. Although mainly a winter visitor some of these birds do nest in this country and remain throughout the year. This is by no means the general rule as the breeding-grounds are in northern European countries, and in late September and during October they arrive on these shores in flocks, resting for a day or so on the coast before journeying inland, where they are most commonly found in remote, hilly districts. When the weather is very severe they come down to the valleys and dells and may be observed in the vicinity of water, especially streams.

The Woodcock is shy by nature and spends most of the day-time well concealed in thick shrubs and undergrowth, coming out at night to feed. As the food consists of insects, grubs and worms found in the mud at the water's edge, the bill is particularly well adapted for this purpose, being very long so as to enable the bird to probe about in the mud collecting its food.

The head, wings and back are reddish-brown, barred with black, while the under parts are of a lighter, and less reddish, brown with darker brown bars; the eye is large and set well back; bill very long and slender; feet and legs grey.

NEST: As already stated, the nest is not usually found in this country, but when it is discovered will be seen to consist of dead leaves and grass and situated in a hollow in the ground usually on the border of a wood.

EGGS: 4 in number; creamy-white, spotted and blotched with reddish-brown and grey mostly at the larger end. (Plate 17, fig. 1a).

COMMON TERN (*Sterno hirundo*).
(Plate 17, fig. 4).

Inland waters are sometimes visited by this bird but the usual haunts are by the sea-shore. It belongs to the same family as the Gulls and in appearance and habits very much

PLATE 17.

1.	Woodcock.	1a.	Egg.
2.	Common Gull.	2a.	Egg.
3.	Black-headed Gull.	3a.	Egg.
4.	Common Tern.	4a.	Egg.

resembles these birds, the chief distinguishing feature being the swallow-like wings and tail. It is a typical marine bird with webbed feet but, unlike the majority of sea-birds, possesses an unusually graceful flight, and when in the air the long, slender, pointed wings and much-forked tail constitute the surest means of identification. The Common Tern is a plentiful bird in the southern half of the country. The cry is piercing and sharp and usually uttered only when in flight. The food consists for the most part of small fish which it obtains while swimming on the water; insects, too, are part of its diet as well as small seashore creatures.

The upper parts of the body are grey and the under sides pale grey; the head and neck black and the bill red; feet and legs orange.

NEST: Practically no attempt is made at nest building but the eggs are laid in a shallow hollow in the shingle or sand.

EGGS: 3 in number; pale olive-brown or greenish-grey, spotted and blotched with dark brown and grey. (Plate 17, fig. 4a).

BLACK-HEADED GULL (*Larus ridibundus*).

(Plate 17, fig. 3).

This Gull, unlike the Common Gull, is found all over the country all the year round, the latter being mainly a winter visitor only in the south. It is a smaller species of the Common Gull and essentially a marine bird and plentiful around the coasts as well as inhabiting mouths of rivers. The food consists of small fish and any scraps to be found on the shore, but it is also fond of grubs which have been turned up by the plough and large flocks of these birds are a familiar sight on a newly cultivated field near the coast.

This species is at once distinguished from the Common Gull by the blackness of its head from which it is named, as well as its smaller size. The wings, like the others of its kind, are very long and pointed and its powerful flight is remarkable, insomuch as it is able to fly against a strong head-wind. The wings and back are slate-grey, the rest of the body white; legs and webbed feet red. During the summer months the black on the crown of the head becomes dark, rusty brown.

Nesting always takes place in colonies in a river estuary or in some remote situation where the birds are unlikely to be disturbed.

NEST: Very simply constructed of grass, and sometimes of rushes and placed on the ground.

EGGS: 3 in number; olive-green with dark brown blotches. (Plate 17, fig. 3a).

COMMON GULL (*Larus canus*).
(Plate 17, fig. 2).

In the south of England the Common Gull is a winter visitor only, its breeding-grounds and summer quarters are in extreme northern countries of England and in Scotland, as well as in Ireland where it is often abundant. During the winter when it is in the south, it is not so often seen inland along the rivers as the Black-headed Gull, for its is a true shore-loving bird and usually observed sitting on the water and following a ship some distance from land. Like the last-named species it also delights in following the plough in search of grubs but it rarely ventures far inland. When nearing the nesting season it flies northwards but does not necessarily breed on the coast, but often large colonies select some marshland site a considerable distance inland.

The head and neck are white; back and wings pearly-grey, the longest wing-feathers black with white tips; tail white; under parts of body white; bill yellowish; legs and feet greenish-yellow. In the winter the white head and neck are streaked with brown.

NEST: Composed of seaweed and dry grass, situated on the ground.

EGGS: 3 in number; greenish-buff, blotched and spotted with brown and grey. (Plate 17, fig. 2a).

RAZORBILL (*Alca torda*).
(Plate 18, fig. 2).

A typical sea-bird found only on the coast and where rocks and cliffs are plentiful for it seldom leaves its rocky haunts except when on a hunting expedition. Small fish constitute the diet and to obtain these the bird spends a great deal of time far out at sea, returning to the shore to resume its sentinel position on the rocks.

The Razorbill is a member of the Auk family and somewhat resembles in appearance the now extinct Great Auk. The plumage of the head, back and wings is black with a greenish reflection; the throat brownish; under parts white. The most characteristic feature is the flattened bill which is strong and very prominent.

It breeds on the ledges of the face of rocks, towering above the sea wall out of reach of all intrusion.

NEST: None, the egg being placed on a ledge of rock.

EGG: 1 only; creamy-white, spotted and blotched with reddish-brown and blackish-brown. (Plate 18, fig. 2a).

GUILLEMOT (*Lomvia troile*).

(Plate 18, fig. 1).

Guillemots are always found in colonies and on some occasions these colonies number many hundreds of birds. At one time they were common all round the coasts of the British Isles but their numbers have somewhat decreased in the south although still inhabiting some of the more unfrequented stretches of coast line. Northwards they become more numerous, being most abundant off the coasts of northern England, and in Scotland and Ireland. When breeding Guillemots congregate in vast numbers on rocky parts of the coast and packed so closely together they often appear a black mass when seen from a distance against the white rocks. When the breeding season is over the birds separate into small colonies and take to the open sea, returning to the communal breeding sites in the following spring.

They feed principally on fish and are expert divers, using their short, strong wings as fins when swimming under water.

From a distance the Guillemot appears a black and white bird but actually the head, neck and back are very dark brown; wings of similar colour but with a narrow white bar; under parts of body white; legs and webbed feet green; bill long and straight and sharply pointed, black in colour.

PLATE 18.

1. Guillemot.	1a.	Egg.
2. Razorbill.	2a.	Egg.
3. Puffin.	3a.	Egg.
4. Moorhen.	4a.	Egg.

NEST: None, the egg is placed on a ledge of rock.

EGGS: 1 only; very variable in colouring, the most usual form being pale green, spotted and blotched with black or dark brown or reddish-brown. (Plate 18, fig. 1a).

PUFFIN (*Fratercula arctica*).
(Plate 18, fig. 3).

Most plentiful on the Farne Islands and less abundant along the east coasts of Scotland and England, but occurs in certain unfrequented stretches of coast in fewer numbers along the south coast. Like the Guillemot and Razorbill, the Puffin is a seashore bird inhabiting rocky coasts and rarely venturing very far inland as its food consists entirely of fish and various marine creatures. It is a squat bird and may be recognized by its extraordinary large bill which is a massive structure, brightly coloured and quite distinct to this species. In the breeding season Puffins congregate in colonies similar to Guillemots and break up into small colonies for the rest of the year. When not engaged in a fishing expedition they sit on the ledges of rocks always facing the sea and often remain motionless for hours on end.

The under parts are black; the face white, under parts of body also white; legs and webbed feet red. The massive bill is bright red on the front half and bluish at the base with a thin strip of bright yellow separating the red and blue, the bill is, therefore, tri-coloured.

NEST: None, the eggs being placed on a ledge of cliff or in a short burrow in the turf at the top of a cliff.

EGGS: 1 only ; dull whitish, sometimes with a few very pale blocks of pale-brown or grey. (Plate 18, fig. 3a).

MOORHEN (*Gallinula chloropus*).
(Plate 18, fig. 4).

The Moorhen is a member of the Coot family and is also known as the Moor-coot or Water-hen. Its natural haunts are in the neighbourhood of marshlands, ponds and streams, and more especially where thick undergrowth will provide plenty of cover. It is a shy bird and when approached, immediately leaves the water or feeding ground and disappears among the foliage. It is equally at home in the water or on land.

When seen from a distance it somewhat resembles a duck, especially when on the water with its head and neck nodding as it swims; diving for food also gives it the appearance of these birds, but a closer inspection will, however, reveal the pointed bill at once distinguishing it from a duck. The Moorhen only flies when alarmed, in order to reach cover more quickly, and when on land its long legs enable it to walk with extraordinary rapidity. The cry is very mellow in tone and is something of a musical note, roughly interpreted as " Croo-og." Its food consists of worms and grubs obtained at the water's edge as well as small aquatic creatures from the bottom of the pond.

Above the colouring is olive-brown; under parts of body slate-grey; the head and neck are also grey; legs and feet yellow. It is very similar in appearance to the Coot but can always be distinguished by the red plumage on the forehead; in the Coot this is white.

NEST: Composed of reeds and dry herbage; it is a bulky structure sometimes placed on the ground among the herbage near the water's edge but not infrequently in rushes growing in the water, but a common nesting site is in a low branch of a tree overhanging a pond, or stream.

EGGS: 7 to 9 in number; pale buff, blotched and spotted with reddish-brown. The young chicks take to the water almost at once and are a very familiar sight during the spring months as they swim after the parent birds. (Plate 18, fig. 4a).

COOT (*Fulica atra*).
(Plate 19, fig. 3).

Very similar in appearance to the Moorhen and found in the same localities as the latter bird, that is, on ponds and lakes and along streams, as it is a typical fresh-water bird. It is two inches longer than the Moorhen but this difference will scarcely suffice in distinguishing the two birds especially when they possess the same dark colouring all over. The distinguishing feature of the Coot is, however, a very conspicuous white, bony plate on the forehead which can be seen clearly when the bird is observed at close quarters. Like the Moorhen the Coot is generally distributed throughout the country being found on inland waters almost everywhere. The note is somewhat harsher than that of the Moorhen, being a sharp " Hawk " usually uttered once only, especially when disturbed. It rarely flies, using its wings only when alarmed and then not rising more than a few feet into the air. When rising from the water it flaps its wings on the surface and drags its long, outstretched legs in the water for some distance before finally taking to the air. Worms, grubs and small aquatic insects obtained from the bottom of the pond are the Coot's favourite foods. Throughout the spring and summer months these birds are usually seen in pairs but during the winter they associate in small flocks, feeding together on mud-flats.

Seen from a distance the Coot appears to be black, but on closer inspection the plumage will be seen to be dark slate-grey above and black on the under parts of the body; forehead with white, bony plate; wings dark grey, almost black, and with a thin white bar across each; legs greenish; bill pinkish-white.

NEST: Made of reeds, rushes and dry grass, situated among the herbage near the water or on a tuft of rushes on the bank of a stream.

EGGS: 7 to 10 in number; buff, spotted with dark brown and blotched with reddish-brown. (Plate 19, fig. 3a).

RED GROUSE (*Lagopus scoticus*).
(Plate 19, fig. 2).

The Red Grouse is a northern inhabitant of these Isles being found most commonly in Scotland and in the northern counties of England as well as in Ireland. It is a typical bird of the moors and dwells in the wildest parts of the country and is very plentiful in some localities where it may be observed in its familiar haunts year after year. The flight of the Red Grouse is not unlike that of the Partridge for, on being disturbed it rises from the ground with whirring wings, flying very strongly in a straight forward direction, skimming

PLATE 19.

1. Partridge.   1a. Egg.
2. Red Grouse.   2a. Egg.
3. Coot.   3a. Egg.
4. Pheasant.   4a. Egg.

92

over the bushes and coming to earth again some distance away. For the most part it is a grain-eater but has also a varied diet consisting of moorland plants and is particularly fond of heather; berries are also eaten when in season. Unlike many game-birds of this order it has only one mate and not several.

A characteristic feature of the Red Grouse is the distinct change of plumage in the summer and winter. During the breeding season the male bird has chestnut-brown back and wings; the head and neck being of a more reddish tinge; breast very dark brown, almost black and flicked with white. The winter plumage is altogether paler and the whitish markings are much more numerous. The female, both in summer and winter is of a lighter hue.

NEST: Composed of leaves, a few sticks and moss, and lined with heather; it is always situated on the ground and is not an elaborate structure.

EGGS: 8 to 10 in number; dirty white, blotched and spotted with reddish-brown. (Plate 19, fig. 2a).

PARTRIDGE (*Perdix cinerea*).
(Plate 19, fig. 1).

The Partridge is the most plentiful of all the game-birds, and is found throughout the country. Mostly it keeps to the open country and is frequently seen in the neighbourhood of cultivated land as it feeds chiefly on grain. Whether in flight or on the ground it is always easy to identify owing to the peculiar downward curve of the wings while in flight, and the general shape of the body.

The Partridge is squat and plump, with a short tail and rounded wings; the bill is short and strong. Reddish-brown is the prevailing colour of the male, the under parts of the body and breast being of a greyish-brown. A characteristic feature is a curious patch of reddish-brown in the shape of a horseshoe situated on the lower part of the breast. The female does not possess this horseshoe marking and the plumage is generally less brown and more inclined to grey.

When alarmed it rises with a loud cackle and whirls away across the meadows or fields, keeping close to the ground.

NEST: Composed of dry grass in a depression in the ground; usually under cover of an overhanging branch of a bush. The hen bird is not always so careful in selecting such a concealed spot, but relies upon her close resemblance to her surroundings, which make her extremely difficult to detect.

EGGS: 10 to 15 in number, sometimes more; plain olive-brown, somewhat pointed. (Plate 19, fig. 1a).

PHEASANT (*Phasianus colchicus*).
(Plate 19, fig. 4).

Next to the Partridge this beautiful-looking bird is the commonest game-bird in Britain, being found in nearly all wooded districts and on downlands which afford sufficient cover. The food consists largely of grain, therefore cultivated land planted with crops and well surrounded by woods, or bracken-covered hillsides, are the most favourite haunts of this most esteemed table-bird. The alarm cry of the male is of a somewhat startling nature when heard close to, and can best be described as a particularly harsh cackle.

The gay plumage of the male renders it at once recognisable. From a distance the general colouring is a brilliant copper but when seen closer the back and wings will be seen to be elaborately marked with black, brown and purple; the head is beautifully coloured and has a wonderful metallic effect of a mixture of blue, green and yellow. The cheeks are red and the long tail and tops of the pointed wings also have numerous crossbars of red and black; the tail in the case of the male accounts for at least eighteen inches of the entire length of the bird. The female is much less gaily adorned and the tail considerably shorter.

In nesting habits the Pheasant closely resembles the Partridge, choosing a concealed spot on the ground among bracken, or in dense undergrowth just inside a wood.

NEST: Not much attempt is made at constructing a nest but a depression in the ground is selected and substantially lined with grass and leaves.

EGGS: 10 to 14 in number; delicate olive-brown without any markings. (Plate 19, fig. 4a).

INDEX.